CONTENTS

This document is not intended to be a comprehensive review of all recent legal developments in this field, or to cover all aspects of those referred to. Readers should take legal advice before applying the information contained in this publication to specific issues or problems.

Foreword

Like all the best team managers (or should I say managers of the best teams), I have a glittering array of talent at my disposal. I am indeed fortunate to be able to call on these talents to produce this short work at the request of The Stationery Office.

The Stationery Office came to us for this purpose after we sent that organisation a copy of our booklet, *Doing Business Electronically*, which we at Ashurst's had published. This was a work primarily prepared by Louise Krosch, who has co-edited this book with me, and Chris Coulter, one of the booklet's contributors. In what now seems like an act of some perspicacity, we took the decision to produce the booklet somewhat ahead of the recent explosion in e-commerce (which even just a couple of years ago was rarely featured on the business pages of any of the broadsheets) in recognition of our clients' need to know not only what the Internet is and how it might or might not be regulated, but what the actual legal issues are in doing business over it. This work builds on that booklet and I hope will be a useful contribution to the growing range of information in this area.

Now for the team list. In the preparation of this work I would like to thank Chris Coulter who was primarily responsible for Chapter 3, Lars Davies who was primarily responsible for Chapter 8 and partly responsible for Chapter 2, Richard Palmer, our tax man, who is responsible for Chapter 7, James Perry who is responsible for Chapter 10, and Charmian May and Richard Cumbley who were jointly responsible for Chapter 11. The remainder of the work was primarily written by Louise Krosch with contributions from a number of us.

We would welcome your comments on this work. If you have comments (hopefully constructive!), please send them to <cmt@ashursts.com>.

Mark Lubbock
29 February 2000

CHAPTER 1

· ·

What is electronic commerce?

With electronic commerce, the world is on the threshold of a new revolution. Because electronic commerce provides a fundamentally new way of conducting commercial transactions, it will have far-reaching economic and social implications. Current ways of doing business will be profoundly modified. – OECD Policy Brief No. 1 (1997).[1]

It has been predicted that Internet electronic commerce will be worth €200 billion a year by the year 2002, of which roughly 80 per cent will comprise supplies to businesses and the rest to consumers. Indeed, even in the short time since the OECD statement in 1997, there has been an enormous growth in the number of Internet users and an explosion in the stock values of companies providing Internet access and Internet directory information. Internet customer loyalty is being bought with business strategies which appear to fly in the face of traditional business methodology. We have stepped over the threshold and the revolution has already begun.

This book examines electronic commerce (or 'e-commerce' as it is more popularly known) conducted over the Internet. There are other ways of doing business electronically – for example, EDI (electronic data interchange) has been around for many years. However, it is Internet e-commerce which is rapidly overtaking all other forms of electronic commerce and it is Internet e-commerce about which the most hype and confusion exists.

The US Treasury has defined e-commerce as:

any transaction involving the exchange of goods and services between two or more parties using electronic tools and techniques.[2]

Common types of e-commerce transactions include:

- *acquiring a product through a website catalogue* – for example, a customer wishing to buy a book can access Amazon Books through its website, order the book and have the book physically delivered

- *downloading computer software* – for example, the customer may wish to order 'Word-Processing for the 21st Century', a software program, and the customer can access the appropriate website, order and take physical delivery of, say, the CD-ROM (as above) or he or she can download the software from the Internet directly onto his or her PC

- *database retrieval* – for example, the legal information database Lexis allows customers to retrieve information from its own proprietary database for a fee, based typically on time spent or the number of searches

- *on-line service provision* – for example, legal services such as the formation of companies, and medical services such as diagnostic services, can be provided over the Internet; similarly, customers can subscribe to the *Wall Street Journal* and customise the types of articles which they want to read.

These types of transactions, which by virtue of the Internet can take place across geographical boundaries, throw up a demanding range of legal and taxation issues, notwithstanding the enduring misapprehension that business conducted over the Internet is under-regulated or not regulated at all. In fact, if anything, the opposite is true. There is no single law of the Internet; as a result of the global nature of the medium, meaning that a supplier's website may potentially be accessed by customers in every jurisdiction, that website may (in theory) be subject to the laws of every country in the world. It is also the case that trading over the Internet raises a large number of legal and commercial questions which businesses have not previously had to face. However, through the application of existing laws and the diligent monitoring of national and international initiatives in the field of e-commerce, businesses can (and must) put themselves into a position where they are able to take advantage of the new revolution.

This book sets out to provide a framework for understanding Internet e-commerce (or 'm-commerce' if carried out using mobile phones) and to review the principal English law issues which anyone intending to conduct business electronically should consider in order to avoid the pitfalls.

Notes

1. OECD Policy Brief No. 1, 1997, available at <www.oecd.org/publications/Pol_brief/9701_Pol.htm>.

2. 'Selected Tax Policy Implications of Global Electronic Commerce', US Treasury Department White Paper 1996, available at <www.ustreas.gov/tax policy>.

CHAPTER 2

The Internet

What is the Internet?

The Internet is a global network of computer networks all speaking the same language. This expanding network of connected networks includes private and public networks, local and wide-area networks, and regional and national networks. The common language used by the computers connected to the Internet is in fact a suite of communication rules or protocols commonly referred to as Internet Protocol, or 'IP'.

The Internet uses packet-switch technology to send data around the various networks. This means that messages are divided into separate packets of data which are then transmitted one at a time, rather than in a continuous stream. When all of the data packets reach their end destination, they are reconstituted to form the original message. One of the efficiency benefits of packet switching is that individual data packets can be sent to the same destination by different routes. This may be useful if a particular route becomes busy or unusable.

These methods of enabling computers to talk to one another and switching messages, which are at the heart of today's Internet, evolved from a 1960s US defence project to create a telecommunications network which could survive a physical assault on a part of the network and still remain operative. The technology was then adopted and developed by academic institutions as a method of communication. However, although (or perhaps because) the Internet grew from a cooperation between the US government and academic society, there is no single organisation which owns or controls the Internet today. Instead, many organisations across the world, both public and private, separately own component parts of the Internet.

Every computer connected to the Internet has a unique electronic numerical IP address called a uniform resource locator or 'URL'. Since long strings of numbers are fairly difficult to remember, the IP address has a unique literary equivalent which is called a domain name and which is allocated (currently) by one of the Internet domain name registries.

Today, users mainly access the Internet via a PC using either a modem and telephone line or, more commonly for businesses, a direct leased line connection to the Internet. However, alternative methods of access to the Internet look likely to become widely available, such as access via a domestic television, and by mobile phone (through the Wireless Application Protocol or 'WAP').

If you think of the Internet as a growing global infrastructure whose parts are owned by many different players, each sending packets of data to one another on the basis of mutual cooperation and using communication standards agreed by custom, you have a rough idea of the way the Internet works today.

The World Wide Web

The World Wide Web, or the web, though probably the most public and recognisable face of the Internet, is not a network at all. Rather, it is a service provided over the Internet infrastructure. Other services available over the Internet include email and usenet (a world-wide discussion medium). However, the web is where a website home page sits and where a 'surfer' visiting a site is likely to find commerce, information and entertainment in a simple and accessible format.

The web is a collection of documents in electronic form which may be viewed by anyone with an Internet connection and appropriate browser software. These documents, written in HTML (hypertext mark-up language), are commonly referred to as web pages. On a page, hypertext links (which exploit a communication protocol called HTTP – Hypertext Transfer Protocol) allow users to navigate to other parts of a page, or to other pages anywhere on the web, simply by clicking on the specified text or graphics.

CHAPTER 3

. . . .

Setting up shop – how and where

Introduction

Once a business has resolved to establish an Internet presence, there will be a number of threshold decisions it needs to make. For example, should the website be a glorified advertisement or electronic brochure, or should it be a fully integrated transaction platform supplementing or even replacing existing ways of doing business? At the start of the process, it is important to remember that all businesses need not necessarily follow the same path – some businesses will be more technologically or logistically able to adapt to doing business electronically than others.

This chapter considers some of the relationships which a business thinking about trading over the Internet may need to establish, and some of the issues which should be explored before formalising those relationships.

Strategy

As with any new business development, the new entrant to the web needs to consider how each of the relationships with its suppliers and partners fits within the overall plan. Getting on the web and making the web work for your business is a project which must be properly managed in order to ensure compatibility and future growth. This may result in a careful review of the structure of the business and, in the case of each of the relationships discussed below, it will be important to consider how each fits in with the business's overall strategy and whether the contracts enshrining those relationships work together. These issues are especially relevant in the Internet world, where the provider of one service or product to a business may also want, or at least be able, to provide services offered by other business partners.

Building a website (design and development)

To establish a web presence, a business needs a website. Many specialist design agencies offer website design services which cover not only how the site looks but also what it can do and how it is structured. Internet service providers (ISPs) and organisations offering hosting services may also offer website design services, possibly as part of an Internet access package.

The 'look and feel' of the website will need to be compatible with your business as a whole and there will be other commercial and marketing issues you will wish to take into account. However, regardless of who designs and develops your website, you will need to address some basic principles:

- *Structure* – The way in which the website is structured and, in particular, the way in which information is presented to the visitor may have significant legal implications. Issues such as contract formation and data protection are discussed below. The website must not only look good and contain the right information, but it must also present that information in the right way.

- *Specifications, delivery and acceptance* – Website design and development is, in essence, a type of software development and, particularly in the context of a coordinated launch project, traditional software development issues will be essential. Accordingly, you should always ensure:

  - compatibility with current browsers and sound and video software – a great-looking site is of no use if only a limited number of visitors can use it or even see it

  - specifications are precise and comprehensive but are flexible enough to allow development

  - delivery obligations are clear and timing can be monitored – avoid the sudden surprise on the due date for delivery

  - acceptance criteria are measurable and acceptance is actual not deemed.

- *Rights clearances* – As with other multimedia works and advertising products, websites might use works in which third parties own copyright or other rights, for example, photographs, text, music or graphics. It is important either to acquire ownership of or a licence to use these works from the rights owner. Given the globally accessible nature of the web, rights clearances should be world-wide, but this may simply not be practical or cost-effective. So major markets should be searched and, if possible, the website designer made responsible for the material it provides, backed up by appropriate indemnities. However, it is important to remember that indemnities are only as valuable as the organisation giving them.

- *Trade marks* – New logos or modifications of existing trade marks may arise as a result of the website development process. Do not assume that your existing trade mark registration(s) will cover the modified Internet version or cover the use of existing marks made in the site. Further trade mark searches of new logos should be carried out well in advance.

- *Ownership of original works* – Rights in original works in the website should be assigned to you. This might apply to (amongst other things) text, graphics or sounds and will also apply to some of the software used in the website. As with other rights, third-party or non-bespoke software used to run the website should be licensed on terms which will enable the site to be continually developed and maintained (and not necessarily by the original developer). This might mean obtaining access to source code or ensuring that readily available tools are used in the development of the website.

Putting your website on the web (hosting)

Once your website is designed and delivered to your satisfaction, it needs to be made accessible to third parties via the Internet: you need to enter into an agreement with a 'host'. A host is essentially a business which operates a computer server attached to the web which will store your website in spare memory and may provide additional services, including updating and amending your website. This host may be the original designer or perhaps an ISP which is also providing you with Internet access.

Some of the issues you will need to address in the relationship with your host will be aimed at ensuring that visitors to your website are presented with a high-calibre product, which reflects the quality of your business:

- *Speed of access* – If your website is slow to load (this might especially be a risk if your website uses 'Rich Media', such as sounds or moving images), visitors may not linger to see what you have to sell. There may be a number of reasons for slow loading. However, one specific element to cover in the contract will be the bandwidth and method of connection used by the host. Where possible and appropriate, it is important to ensure that a high-bandwidth direct ISDN connection is used to support your website.

- *Server response* – Other factors may affect the performance of your website and these should all be covered by appropriate contractual obligations. Issues to be covered will include server memory space, the number of other hosted clients and anticipated traffic to your site. A guaranteed performance level based on system uptime should also be considered.

- *Reporting* – Statistical information relating to site usage can be vital when targeting customers in a competitive environment. You should ensure that your host can provide such information in a form you can use.

- *Disaster recovery* – You should check that backup facilities are available and whether the host runs a standby service.

- *Security* – You must consider the level of security that the host offers in respect of your data. This issue is of particular concern where you are processing personal data, such as customer details.

- *Compatibility* – Where your website is an interactive platform enabling commercial transactions, you should also ensure that the host's systems are compatible with your e-commerce platform software.

- *Economies of scale* – Where you also run extensive voice networks, it may be cost-efficient to arrange for your own direct circuit rental for Internet traffic. However, it is important to ensure that support contracts do not leave you exposed – try to avoid the danger of multiple service providers being able to avoid liability by blaming someone else.

Where on the web? (portals, gateways and other partners)

Although there are no physical geographical boundaries on the web, there are still sites which are more popular than others. You will wish to register site details with major search engines such as Yahoo! and Infoseek and you may consider employing technical devices such as metatags (which flag up the site to search engines) in your web design.

However, the web today is witnessing the emergence of new intermediaries which may be highly relevant to your business. Key players in the commercial evolution of the Internet are expected to be the portals. There is some debate as to whether particular organisations are portals, gateways or merely ISPs providing value-added services. In this book, reference to a portal means a website which provides space for other businesses to market their products and permits links to the websites of those businesses. Sometimes the portal site will be divided into 'channels' such as 'financial', 'entertainment' and 'shopping' channels, thereby segmenting its resident businesses into different categories for the ease of the visitor. Organisations such as Virgin Net, Yahoo!, Microsoft Network (MSN), AOL and Freeserve all offer variations on the portal theme.

When entering into such a relationship you should consider issues such as:

- *Network performance* – As with hosting agreements, the technical capabilities and performance of the portal may be highly significant to the value of the portal.

- *Branding* – Establishing an Internet-trusted brand is one of the key factors to successful e-commerce. You should ensure that the use of your trade marks by portal partners is compatible with your overall strategy and consider what other products or services are being offered alongside yours: association with competitors may not necessarily be detrimental but you may not want your children-oriented products sold alongside, for example, adult services.

- *Exclusivity* – The level of exclusivity offered by the portal owner should be considered. For example, you should ask whether your site will be the only site selling to your customer market.

- *'On-screen' positioning* – You should investigate where the references to your business will be positioned on the portal. It is important to remember that, from a commercial perspective, what the visitor sees first on his or her screen may be key to sales.

- *Visitor data* – Some portals will seek to capture and 'own' the information relating to the visitors to your site. This may be reasonable or not, depending on the circumstances, but is an important issue particularly if, at some time, you may wish to change portals.

Don't forget the real world (integration and fulfilment)

Finally, depending upon the nature of your existing business, you will need to consider the real-world issue of how your website and e-commerce transactions relate to your pre-existing business systems and ask the following questions:

- *Financial* – Where payment is being received on-line, are arrangements (including those relating to security) with banks and credit card companies in place?

- *Integration* Has your web business been integrated with your existing computer systems and databases? Interface systems may need to be developed in order to maximise the benefit of your existing systems; are development services covered by your existing support contracts?

- *Distribution* – With the exception of digital products which can be downloaded directly from your website, there is a real need for efficient order processing and fulfilment – this means comprehensive distribution arrangements covering the markets you expect to service.

  For the seller accustomed to over-the-counter trading, important business relationships and new sale and distribution channels will need to be negotiated. Are these in place or in train?

- *Customer care and support* – What happens if your website crashes or visitors have either technical or transaction-related enquiries? Do your existing technical support contracts provide or permit a satisfactory customer interface, or are they designed to cater for supplier-to-seller support?

CHAPTER 4

Contracting over the Internet

Contract basics

There are four main requirements for any binding contract under English law: an offer, an acceptance of that offer, consideration and an intention to create legal relations. Contracts need not be in writing or in any particular form to be enforceable – they can be oral or made by an exchange of correspondence and, under English law, can be made in a number of different media including paper, air, telephone wires and over the Internet.

There is much academic debate about the precise ambit of consideration. However, in short, consideration must be 'something of value in the eye of the law'.[1] This might include the mutual exchange of promises and need not necessarily be payment of money. The Internet does not present any substantial new issues in this context although it does provide a platform for new payment mechanisms such as digital cash. Making clear what consideration is given remains as important on the Internet as in traditional marketplaces.

Similarly, existing law on intention may be applied to the Internet. Ever since Lord Denning[2] made clear that a contract could be completed by a machine (in that case, an automatic ticket dispenser), it has been clear that software could perform the functions of, say, a seller. Provided that no lack of intention on the seller's part is made known to the buyer, the lack of direct human intention in each case will not be an obstacle to formation of a contract. Therefore, this chapter focuses on the issues of offer and acceptance where the Internet raises some novel issues. We also look at methods of ensuring that contractual terms and conditions are incorporated into contracts made over the Internet. Finally, we look briefly at some jurisdictional issues raised by contracting over a global medium and at the proposals made in the EC Directive on certain legal aspects of e-commerce in relation to contracting.[3]

What is an offer?

English law distinguishes between 'offers' (which can be accepted to form a contract) and 'invitations to treat'. An invitation to treat is essentially where A invites B to make an offer which A is then free to accept or reject. On the Internet, this distinction raises two interesting points.

First, a seller may not wish to be contractually bound to every person who visits its website. The seller may simply not have enough stock to meet demand or there may be geographical obstacles, such as where a New York pizza delivery service finds itself contractually obliged to deliver pizza to a hungry customer in London.

Even where questions of demand, supply and physical delivery are not an issue (for example, in sale or licence of 'digital products' such as software or music), there may be other reasons why the seller might not wish to be bound to every potential buyer. The seller may be operating under a licence which forbids it from selling in certain territories or there may be problems of local law compliance (for example, it may be unlawful for a seller to export certain goods to certain specified territories, or the sale of those goods may be prohibited or regulated in the buyer's territory).

So a web-based seller should make every effort to demonstrate that it is only making an invitation to treat. Clear language is the key. Sellers should consider including a statement that the seller will not be bound unless and until the seller accepts, by a specified means, communications from potential buyers. Sellers should also bear in mind that statements which are never read by potential buyers (because they do not form a necessary part of the on-line purchasing process) will not help persuade a court that the website was intended as an invitation. Here, then, sellers need to consider the actual manner in which their website is used, ensuring that each step in the contract formation process is mirrored by clear, non-avoidable, statements on its website.

This section examines the mechanism of contract formation, rather than the content of an Internet contract. However, a seller will want to ensure that its own unamended terms and conditions are incorporated into any contract it enters into with a buyer. This is complicated by the fact that the seller may well wish to set up its site in such a manner that acceptance is effected by an automatic computerised process. Thus, the second issue to consider when making an Internet invitation is how to structure the offer so that the buyer presents to the seller the offer the seller is expecting. In effect, the seller is inviting the buyer to make an offer on the basis of the seller's terms and conditions. When the buyer 'accepts' this premise (and presumably provides additional identity or payment information), the seller must ensure, by using appropriate software, that the buyer's response/offer is limited to a 'yes/no' choice. There must be no opportunity for the buyer to amend the terms in a way which may not be picked up by the seller's software.

What is acceptance?

Acceptance of the terms of an offer is what brings a contract into existence. Generally speaking, the acceptance of an offer must be 'unconditional' (that is, on the same terms as the original offer) and must be communicated to the offeror. In addition, an offer may normally be revoked at any time up to the point of acceptance. So the timing of acceptance and the answer to the question 'When is the contract formed?' are critical.

Traditionally, there have been two rules used to determine when acceptance has occurred and it is not yet clear which rule, if either, will apply to Internet transactions.

As a general rule, where acceptance is given by instantaneous communication (such as face-to-face or by telephone), acceptance is deemed to have been communicated to the offeror when it is received by the offeror. There is, however, an important exception to the general rule, known as the postal rule, where acceptance is given by a delayed form of communication such as by post. In this situation, acceptance is deemed to take place upon posting of the letter of acceptance (although this is rebuttable, if, for example, the person sending the acceptance knew that the postal service was disrupted).

It is worth remembering one of the reasons why there is a special rule for communications by post or telegram. The people using these methods of communication are entrusting their messages to an independent third party, such as the Post Office, who the two parties have impliedly agreed should be entrusted with the message.

However, as mentioned in Chapter 2, there is no single person in charge of the Internet. Therefore, following traditional law and looking upon the Internet as providing a form of instantaneous communication, it might seem that the acceptance by the seller would not occur until the buyer receives notice of the acceptance. Further, if the contract is formed only when and where acceptance is received by the buyer, then for global transactions where the seller is in the UK and the buyer is in Germany or the US and there is no express choice of law, it may become more difficult to determine which law (English, German, or US state or federal law) applies to the contract. This might not be satisfactory for an e-commerce seller who wants to know when its obligations have become binding, when it can recognise revenues, and which laws apply. However, for Internet contracts, it also helps to look at the technology involved. This highlights some differences between email and 'website-based' communication.

Although there is little direct case law, it is possible that courts may view contracts concluded 'at' a website as different from contracts concluded by the exchange of email. This is because with most website-based contracts there will be a direct and 'real-time' link between the visitor and host. If the direct link is lost, both parties should become aware of that fact almost immediately. So, like fax, a website offer and acceptance probably amounts to what is effectively instantaneous communication and does not take place until acceptance is received by the offeror.

By contrast with website-based contracts, email is (notoriously) not an instantaneous communication method; but this does not necessarily mean that the postal rule will apply. The answer to which rule applies in the case of email transactions may depend upon the circumstances in a given situation. That is, one may need to identify where in the network of computers which is the Internet the transaction actually takes place. So, for example, a different result may be achieved if a contract is to be formed between a buyer and seller doing business through a common server (in which case it might be that the postal rule applies – both parties having impliedly agreed to use a shared method of communication) as opposed to where each party has its own mail server (in which case the general rule may well apply). It may also be that the contract is formed in a server not known to the buyer or seller, somewhere in the Internet, and possibly not in the jurisdiction of either buyer or seller.

The practical solution when setting up an Internet transaction is to assess in advance the mechanics of the contract formation process and, armed with that information, to specify in advance how offer and acceptance can be given. In particular, the point at which acceptance occurs must be specified. From the perspective of the seller, three things will need to be made very clear. First, messages are only valid when they are received (and specifying what 'received' means will also need to be precise – it could mean by mail server or by human operator, depending upon the e-commerce system). Second, the seller will want to be equally clear when acceptance takes place (that is, when the contract is actually formed) since, from this point on, all obligations become binding upon the parties. Third, the seller will need to ensure that it does not accept the offer until it is sure it can comply with its obligations and it should make it clear that receipt of confirmation of the order does not necessarily equate to acceptance.

Which laws apply?

As discussed briefly above, the way in which offers and acceptances are given over the Internet may mean that a contract is formed in a jurisdiction other than the seller's home territory. Even if it is formed in the seller's home territory, there may be overriding rules of law in some jurisdictions which apply to the contracts made, no matter where the contract is formed. Some of these laws are discussed in the following sections.

When looking at the law which governs an on-line contract, the general rule under English law is that the parties to a contract can choose which law should govern that contract. For most types of contract, the applicable law is decided irrespective of the other party's location, under the UK Contracts (Applicable Law) Act 1990 (the 1990 Act). This implements the Rome Convention, an EC Convention which determines the issue of the law which should govern contractual obligations between two EU parties. The 1990 Act will almost always uphold an express or implied choice of law in a contract. In inferring a choice of law, a UK court will look at a variety of factors including previous dealings between the parties, references in the agreement to payments in a particular currency or the statutes of a particular country.

If there is no choice of law clause (either express or implied), a contract will be governed by the laws of the country with which it has the closest connection. However, consumer contracts will often be governed by the law of the consumer's country of habitual residence.

In order to reduce the risk that a court would impose an unexpected choice of law, although it does not guarantee that it will be applied, sellers should always state an appropriate applicable law – for UK businesses, this is usually English but could be Scottish law. However, even if the contracting parties make a choice of law, that choice cannot deprive consumers of the protection of any mandatory national laws of the country where they have their habitual residence. Therefore, when dealing with consumers, sellers should always ensure that terms and conditions (including any exclusions of liability) provide an adequate level of consumer protection. This is certainly the case under English law.

Apart from the law which should govern the contract itself, a seller should also prescribe the jurisdiction where contractual disputes should be dealt with. Every country has a private international law which forms part of the laws of that country. These rules are used to identify the court which should have jurisdiction in the event of a dispute with parties located in different jurisdictions. They may override the parties' choice of jurisdiction, but in most cases other than those identified below they will not, and the parties' choice will generally be respected if it is challenged later.

In the UK, the Brussels Convention applies to disputes between parties domiciled in the EU and the Lugano Convention applies to disputes between parties domiciled in the European Economic Area (EEA). Where one of the parties is domiciled elsewhere (for example, the United States or Japan), English common law rules of jurisdiction will apply.

Under these conventions, special rules apply to consumer contracts by virtue of the fact that consumers are recognised at law as being in an unequal bargaining position. Notwithstanding a choice of jurisdiction clause in a supplier's terms and conditions, under the Brussels and Lugano Conventions a consumer is entitled to bring proceedings either where he or she is domiciled or where the supplier is domiciled. Conversely, a consumer may only be sued in the courts of his or her own country.

However, at present, these rules apply only to certain types of consumer contracts, particularly those for the supply of goods or services, where:

- a specific invitation was issued to the consumer in his or her country or the consumer responded to some advertising in that country before the contract was concluded, and

- the consumer took all necessary steps on his or her own part to conclude the contract in that country.

It has long been considered that targeting customers in foreign jurisdictions by sending emails may amount to 'specific invitation'. In contrast, it has been generally assumed that these rules would not apply to a business located in one jurisdiction with a website which is accessed by a person elsewhere.

However, the European Commission recently adopted draft regulations to amend the Brussels Convention, the aim being to create uniform rules of private international law across the EU relating to jurisdiction and to improve the recognition and enforcement of judgments in civil and commercial matters. The draft regulations also seek to strengthen consumer protection laws by enabling consumers to sue in their own courts in relation to all types of contracts, including sales concluded via a website.

The new regulations state that if a company directs activities towards one or several member states, the court of the consumer's country of residence can take jurisdiction in the event of a contractual dispute. The difficulty is that the phrase 'directing activities' may mean that if a foreign consumer accesses a company's website and offers to buy goods or services, the company could be said to have 'directed' its activities towards that consumer's country. This may be so irrespective of whether or not the company intends to target foreign consumers.

The Commission is also proposing new rules for non-contractual liability under what is being called the 'Rome 2 Regulation'. These rules provide that, where a company is established in one member state and trading lawfully under the laws of that state, it may find itself subject to unfair competition laws of another member state if its website can be accessed by consumers in that state. The practical effect of this is that a UK company which is complying with English rules with respect to advertising and promotion may find itself falling foul of foreign unfair competition laws where such advertisements or promotions are illegal.

The proposed changes have caused concern for companies engaging in e-commerce. Their practical effect is that a business may be required to ensure (at least) that the provisions of its website comply with the national laws in each of the 15 EU member states or risk penalty. At the time of writing, the Commission was still considering submissions as to how 'directing activities' should be interpreted. On a practical level, this may mean including different sets of terms and conditions on a website which comply with various local law requirements. For example, contracts with French consumers must be written in French in order to be valid, so it may be necessary for a UK business to include a link on its English-language site to web pages with French-language terms and conditions (drafted also to comply with French consumer protection laws).

The alternative is to use technological measures either to prevent customers from certain jurisdictions accessing a website or to refuse to supply customers from certain jurisdictions. In fact, the Commission has suggested that companies can protect themselves from potential litigation across the various member states of the EU by including specific language on their websites that their products or services cannot be purchased by customers domiciled in particular member states. This language would need to be backed up by the company taking steps to ensure that, notwithstanding the expressed prohibition on sales to such customers, no such supplies were actually made.

The proposals are the subject of considerable controversy. In particular, the proposals and suggested measures to address their effect conflict entirely with the advantages apparent through the use of electronic commerce, making pan-European advertising and promotions impossible. Further, it is often difficult to identify where a consumer who accesses a site is resident, and refusal to supply a party seeking to purchase from a website set up to offer goods or services to nationals of another member state might breach EC competition rules.

It remains to be seen whether lobbying against the proposed regulations will be successful.

Incorporation of terms

In order for the process of contract formation to achieve the seller's objectives, the seller will want to ensure that its terms and conditions are actually incorporated into the contract with the buyer.

Simply put, the seller must bring its terms and conditions sufficiently to the attention of the buyer before the contract is formed and in a manner that does not enable the buyer to make a counter-offer with different terms and conditions. This means displaying the terms and conditions on the website and there are several ways this can be done. At one end of the spectrum, the buyer will be unable to buy (or rather to make the offer to buy) before it has been presented with a suitable warning and, perhaps, an automatic non-avoidable screen which displays the full terms and conditions. It is fairly likely that presentation in this manner will lead to incorporation of terms. However, its commercial acceptability might depend upon the type of transaction contemplated. Clearly, requiring a consumer to scroll down pages of contractual terms and conditions before a purchase can be made could be unattractive in marketing terms to the look and feel of the website. At the other end of the spectrum, an indication that the terms and conditions can be made available on email request or a hypertext link hidden away without reference, may well not be sufficient.

Structuring the website in an order sufficient to bring the applicable terms and conditions to the attention of customers will be an important aspect of the Internet trader's web presence and will involve a sensible commercial and legal risk assessment.

The E-Commerce Directive

The proposed E-Commerce Directive (which at the time of writing is close to adoption) requires EU member states to ensure that their legislation allows contracts to be concluded electronically but allows certain derogations (which are arguably overbroad) as follows:

- contracts requiring the involvement of a notary
- contracts which in order to be valid are required to be registered with a public authority

- contracts governed by family law

- contracts governed by the law of succession.

The first two derogations are in particular so broad as to allow many member states potentially to avoid having to implement the primary obligation of the proposed Directive altogether. As member states are required to provide the European Commission with a complete list of the categories covered by the derogations, the Commission may in future seek to cut down the scope of the derogations.

The proposed Directive also provides that member states will set out in their legislation that the way in which a contract is formed electronically must be explained to customers prior to the conclusion of the contract. It is interesting to note that the Electronic Communications Bill recently published by the HM Government fails to do this.

Finally, the proposed Directive sets out the rules for a particular case where a contract is concluded electronically, that is, in the circumstances where, in accepting an offer, the customer is required to give his or her consent through technological means such as clicking on an icon. The proposed Directive provides that the contract is concluded only when the customer has received from the service provider an electronic acknowledgement of receipt of the customer's acceptance, receipt being defined as the moment at which the recipient of the service is able to access it (in other words, not when the customer actually *does* access it). The extent to which this method of concluding a contract will actually exist in practice is uncertain.

Notes

1. *Thomas v. Thomas* (1842).

2. *Thornton v. Shoe Lane Parking* (1971).

3. Com (1999) 427 final.

CHAPTER 5

Consumer protection

Introduction

One of the problems facing businesses seeking to embrace global e-commerce is that local consumer protection laws may override or supplement stated contract terms. Local compliance checks in major foreign markets will be one prudent step for a business moving from a national to an international platform.

In particular, there are a number of consumer protection laws applicable to businesses operating within the EU which cannot be excluded. So, for example, businesses selling to consumers in the EU will (or ought to) be familiar with the EC Directive on Unfair Terms in Consumer Contracts which was implemented in the UK in 1995. Terms which are unfair are not enforceable and it is easy to see that a term purporting to give English courts exclusive jurisdiction (that is, forcing a consumer to sue in England or Wales) might well be unfair. Furthermore, the applicability of this Directive cannot be avoided by choosing a non-EU law – thus, for example, US businesses selling into the EU also need to be aware of the local laws.

Another such overriding law, which raises some interesting issues in the context of the Internet, is the proposed Distance Selling Directive. There are also some consumer protection provisions in the Directive on certain aspects of e-commerce and other EU Directives, and under the national laws of the EU member states.

The Distance Selling Directive

This EC Directive was agreed in May 1997 for the protection of consumers in respect of distance contracts. 'Distance contracts' include sales concluded through the use of telephones (with or without human intervention), email or fax. Therefore the terms of the Directive are intended to apply to contracts formed over the Internet. The standards prescribed by the Directive are minimum only and must be implemented in the UK by 4 June 2000. However, at the time of writing, no date for the introduction of legislation to bring UK law into line with the Directive has been set. As the burden is on the supplier of the goods and services to prove compliance, it would be prudent for a supplier to ensure that terms and conditions of sale governing any such 'distance contracts' at least comply with the Directive in its current form.

In broad terms, the Directive requires that suppliers provide customers with the following information well before the conclusion of the distance contract:

- the main characteristics of the goods supplied
- all prices (inclusive of tax) to be paid, including delivery costs
- arrangements for payment, delivery or performance
- the costs of using the means of distance communication (where it is calculated other than at the basic rate)
- the address to which the customer may address complaints to the supplier
- information on what after-sale services or guarantees exist.

Generally, customers must be given a right to withdraw from a distance contract within seven business days of receipt by them of goods supplied. While a full refund of the price paid must be given, a supplier is still entitled to charge the customer for the direct costs of returning the goods. There is, however, no right to withdraw for certain categories of goods, including: custom-made goods; perishable goods; periodicals and magazines (although, curiously, books are not included); and audio or video recordings or computer software which have been unsealed by the consumer. In the case of the latter category, suppliers of these items will want to seal these goods prior to despatch in order to take advantage of this exception.

Unless the parties agree otherwise, the supplier must execute each order within a maximum of 30 days from the day the customer 'forwards' the order to the supplier. In the case of on-line contracts, this is arguably the date the customer sends the order to the supplier via email or website (which may not necessarily be the day that the supplier receives the email). Provision should therefore be made for this in any standard terms and conditions of sale. If the goods ordered are unavailable, the customer must be informed of the situation and is entitled to a refund of any sums paid as soon as possible, and in any case within 30 days.

Finally, a customer must be given the right to request cancellation of the payment where a fraudulent use of a payment card has been made and the customer must in that case be re-credited. Although 'payment card' is not defined, this is clearly intended to include credit and debit cards.

Other consumer protection Directives

There are a number of other Directives the principal purpose of which are to protect consumers and which are relevant to electronic commerce. These include:

- the Data Protection Directive
- the Directive on Unfair Terms and Consumer Contracts
- the Misleading Advertising Directive
- the proposed Electronic Commerce Directive.

The Data Protection Directive is discussed in some detail in Chapter 11. The Directive on Unfair Terms and Consumer Contracts requires member states to include in their law provisions rendering unenforceable unfair or unreasonable terms and unreasonable attempts to disclaim or exclude liability. This Directive is to a considerable extent already incorporated in UK law by the Unfair Contract Terms Act 1977. The Misleading Advertising Directive[1] requires member states to implement adequate and effective means to control misleading adverts.

The proposed E-Commerce Directive deals with the liability of information society service providers and with commercial communications which are broadly defined and include advertisements, promotions and so on. The latter of these provide that all commercial communications should be clearly identifiable as such, should identify on whose behalf they are made, and should set out clearly the conditions which need to be met in order for the recipient to qualify for promotional offers, competitions or games which are contained in them. It also deals with unsolicited commercial communications (in other words 'spam') – this is discussed in more detail in Chapter 9. The proposed Directive also purports to provide some protection for information service providers from liability for damages provided that the provider in question does not initiate the transmission, does not select the receiver of the transmission, and does not select or modify the information contained in the transmission.

The intention behind this legislation is to protect those ISPs that merely act as conduits for the transmission of information and do not attempt to influence it in any way. There are also provisions relating to the practices of caching and hosting.

Notes

1. Directive 84/450/EEC as amended by Directive 97/55/EC.

CHAPTER 6

. . . .

Intellectual property aspects

Copyright and database rights

What is copyright?

Copyright is the exclusive right to reproduce certain types of creative works. In the EU, it arises automatically upon the creation of such works without any need for registration and generally lasts 70 years from the death of the author. There is no such thing as an international copyright law, as rights of copyright are based on national legislation. There are, however, a number of international treaties and conventions which seek to harmonise national copyright laws.

Copyright subsists in original literary, dramatic, musical or artistic works, sound recordings, films, broadcasts, cable programmes and certain databases. Literary works include computer programs and the preparatory materials used in creating them. 'Original' does not mean new. It means that the work has been created without copying another work (meaning it is possible that two very similar works can acquire independent copyright).

The Internet is awash with information, including news stories, software, novels, music, screenplays, graphics, artwork and photographs. These are all works protected by copyright. However, copyright is often a bundle of rights and, in the case of material on the Internet, several different copyrights may subsist in what appears to be the one 'work'. For example, a music retailer's on-line trading site may include a broadcast of a snippet from a Boyzone concert. There will be, amongst other things, different copyrights in the broadcast itself, the choreography of the dance routines, the music and the lyrics, the rights to each of which may be owned by a different person. Further, the design of the retailer's web page, being an arrangement of elements such as text, graphics and audio, will (in addition to the rights of copyright in these aspects) also be a copyright work.

How do you protect your copyright works?

Acts which a copyright owner can prevent include copying the work, making adaptations of the work and issuing copies to the public. An infringing act must be in relation to the work as a whole or a substantial part of it.

The act of viewing material on a website causes a temporary copy of the site to be made in the viewer's random access memory (RAM) which may then be printed out, downloaded to disk or saved in the viewer's hard drive. In all of these cases, the viewer has reproduced all or a substantial part of the material, which in theory constitutes infringement of the rights of the copyright owner(s).

Although the point has not yet been considered directly, the UK courts have held that the test as to whether or not a licence to use a copyright work has been implied depends on whether, viewing the facts objectively, the words and conduct of the alleged licensor indicated that the licensor consented to what the licensee was doing. Therefore, in practice, most commentators agree that a licence would be implied to cover much of this sort of copying as the technology in question, by necessity, dictates it will occur. However, it is unclear as to how far this implied licence can extend – thus, for example, whereas a licence to view the material can be implied, a licence to download and print out a hard copy, or even a licence to save it for later review, may not.

It is therefore advisable to include in the terms and conditions of sale or elsewhere on your website the following:

- a copyright statement indicating the extent of your rights in any software, text, images and graphics and in their selection or arrangement
- a statement giving the customer permission to copy electronically and print portions of the site solely for personal use, to place an order or other permitted use
- a statement permitting the customer to make one copy of any software or material which appears on the site for archival or back-up purposes provided that any copy contains all of the original proprietary notices (including the copyright statement).[1]

Third-party copyright

As discussed above, websites use works in which third parties own copyright – for example, photographs, text or graphics – and it is important either to acquire ownership of or a licence to use these works from the copyright owner. In the case of existing licences to use copyright works, it cannot be assumed that they include in their grant of rights permission to copy and use the licensed work on the Internet or in electronic or digital format. Copyright owners are increasingly protesting against unauthorised uploading of their works and UK courts have not yet settled as to whether a licence to print, publish, use or distribute a work implies a right to do so in all media, including the Internet.

Database rights

In addition to copyright, a database may attract protection under the new 'database right' even where it does not have the sufficient level of originality in its selection or arrangement to qualify for copyright protection as a literary work. This new right may be used to prevent the extraction and reuse of certain databases where there has been substantial investment in obtaining, varying or presenting their contents, and it lasts for 15 years. Furthermore, any substantial change to the contents of such a database (including a substantial change resulting from the accumulations of successive deletions and alterations) will qualify the 'new' database for a further 15-year period of protection.

Trade marks

What is a trade mark?

A trade mark is a sign (such as a name or logo) used by a business to distinguish its goods or services from those from another source and may be registered or unregistered. As with copyright, trade mark rights are derived under national laws. In the case of registered trade marks, they are usually registered in respect of specific goods or services at registries in countries where the trade mark owner claims rights (that is, in places where either it or its licensees do or intend to do business). In appropriate circumstances, the owner of either a registered or an unregistered trade mark can take action against third parties to prevent their use of the same mark or a confusingly similar one.

Using your trade marks on the Internet

Although an Internet trader may have trade mark registrations for its trade marks and logos in certain territories, the global nature of the Internet means that in theory the mark is capable of being 'used' in each country in which a visitor is able to access the website, including territories where third parties may have prior existing rights.

For example, a company which sells children's footwear on-line may own rights to the trade mark BOOTIE in the UK, France and Germany and operate the BOOTIE website. The rights to the mark BOOTIE in respect of clothing and footwear may be owned by a third party in Japan. Arguably, if a customer in Japan accesses the BOOTIE website, a trade mark infringement of the Japanese registration occurs when the BOOTIE mark appears on the customer's computer screen in Japan.

In an ideal world, searches should be conducted to obtain a world-wide clearance on the use of your trade marks on the Internet. However, in reality, this is impractical and it would be an extremely costly exercise. At the very least, it is prudent to conduct trade mark searches in those key territories where you intend to do business via the Internet, to check whether there are any prior conflicting rights in those jurisdictions.

It is also advisable to use disclaimers which specify the geographical limitations of the business carried on under the trade mark. The effectiveness of website disclaimers has yet to be considered by the UK courts. However, their use is gathering widespread acceptance in the business community.

Using third-party trade marks

It is legitimate to display goods and services on your website which are 'branded' with third-party trade marks provided it is clear that the reference is to the goods and services of that other party – in the same way that a physical storekeeper displays products on its shelves.

What about domain names?

Domain names

As discussed above, a domain name is a human comprehensible alternative to the IP address used to identify websites on the Internet. The prefix of each domain name identifies the Internet user's host computer and the suffix identifies the nature of the entity (commercial, educational, governmental, etc.) and/or the country of registration. An on-line seller will typically want to include its trading name or trade mark in its domain name (for example, <hmv.co.uk>).

Domain names are allocated on a country-by-country basis by registries set up for that purpose. The same name can be registered in various countries, differentiated only by their country suffix to the name. Significantly, the UK courts have already held that a domain name's reputation and use can have trade mark significance.[2] However, unlike trade marks (where different international classes of goods and services mean that two or more organisations may register the same trade mark covering unrelated classes), there is at present no possibility for different companies to have exactly the same domain name even if they are in completely different areas of business.

Domain name registries generally operate on a 'first come, first served' basis, where two unrelated parties who have legitimate rights to the same or similar trade marks covering different goods or services seek to register an identical domain name. This was the case in *Prince*[3] where a US manufacturer of tennis rackets could not prevent a UK-based IT company's legitimate registration and use of the domain name <prince.com>.

However, this practice should be compared with 'cybersquatting' or 'domain name piracy'. This is the situation where a party with no legitimate claim to a trade mark obtains an opportunistic registration of a domain name incorporating that mark in order to take advantage of the 'first come, first served' policy – with a view to extracting payment for the 'transfer' of the registration to the trade mark proprietor. At least in the UK, it appears well-settled that intentional cybersquatting with respect to well-known and established brands may amount to passing off or an appropriation of the trade mark proprietor's goodwill.[4]

Generally speaking, domain name administration has now been taken over at an international level by Internet Corporation for Assigned Names and Numbers (ICANN), a non-profit organisation based in California. The registration process has been opened up to a number of competing registrars from around the world, each of which has the right to allocate genuine top-level domain names to their customers (for example, .com, .net, .org) provided they are accredited. In addition to allocating domain names, accredited registrars are bound by their agreement with ICANN to offer certain facilities. For example, all domain name agreements incorporate a uniform dispute resolution policy, paving the way for a very quick and impartial resolution for domain name disputes. However, the policy itself does not prevent parties from pursuing their claims in court.

Points to consider when setting up on-line

As with trade marks, it is advisable to conduct international clearance searches to reveal whether any identical registrations or confusingly similar ones exist. You should also consider obtaining domain registrations (preferably for all names used in connection with your on-line business) in the key territories where you intend to do business and in order to mirror your trade mark portfolio. Registration fees are relatively inexpensive (usually between £100 and £200), although these may escalate in the event of a dispute with a third party claiming pre-existing rights. In addition, it may not be possible to get registrations in all such territories as some jurisdictions (such as France) require registrants to be actively trading in the jurisdiction, while others will only permit one registration per applicant.

Linking and framing

What is 'linking'?

As discussed, the World Wide Web uses hypertext mark-up language (HTML) to program its pages. Any HTML document may be linked to another HTML document and these 'hypertext links' allow information from disparate computers around the world to be immediately accessed. Linking enables users to access instantly different pages and different sites anywhere in the world without the need to use complicated Internet addresses.

There are four common website linking practices:

- a link from one website to the home page of another website

- drawing material into one website through a link with another website (so-called 'in-line linking')

- a link from one website to a particular page of another website (so-called 'deep linking')

- a link from one website to the pages of another website whose pages are still 'framed' by the original website; 'framing' operates in a way that, from the user's perspective, the web page location and other windows (which often contain advertising) remain static while the user views other sites through the frames, unaware that he or she is now actually viewing the contents of a third-party site.

It is as yet unsettled by case law as to whether or not express permission is required in every case in order to link to another site. It has been argued that linking to a third-party site involves, amongst other things, copying (or, at least, facilitating the copying of) the material on that site (copyright infringement) and unauthorised use of third-party trade marks or copyrights as the 'link' (for example, in the former case, use of the company logo or name and, in the latter, the use of its URL).

In addition, the context in which the hypertext link to a third-party site is presented may amount to a misrepresentation of an association with the owner of the third-party site or an impression that the site is sponsored or endorsed by the third-party site, which it may be possible to prevent by a trade mark infringement or passing-off action.

In the *Shetland Times* case[5] a Scottish court had occasion to consider deep linking. In that case, the plaintiff had an on-line version of its paper-based newspaper, the *Shetland Times*. The front page of the paper featured headlines for articles contained in subsequent pages, together with advertising. Stories could be accessed by clicking on the headlines. The *Shetland News* reproduced headlines from the *Shetland Times* site, with each headline being hypertext linked to the relevant individual articles in the *Shetland Times* site, thus bypassing the *Shetland Times* home page and advertising located there.

The case was eventually settled. However, in considering whether or not to grant an interim injunction, the Scottish court held that there was a good case that this linking amounted to an infringement of copyright. This was, in part, based on the defendants' concession that a headline could be a literary work and the court's assumption that some of the headlines at issue might constitute copyright works.[6] Using a somewhat curious analysis, the court also found that the headlines were 'cable programmes' (and thus protected by copyright) within the meaning of the UK Copyright Designs and Patents Act 1988, and that the facility available on the defendants' website amounted to a cable programme service which infringed the plaintiff's copyright by including the headlines in that service.

Another case worthy of note, despite being settled, is the US decision in *Ticketmaster Corp v. Microsoft Corp*.[7] Although the terms of the settlement are confidential, Microsoft agreed to cease its practice of bypassing the Ticketmaster home page advertisements and deep linking to a web page within Ticketmaster's website, which offered on-line ticket purchasing facilities.

In other cases in the United States, for example *Futuredontics Ltd v. Applied Anagramatics*,[8] action has been taken in relation to 'framing'.

Linking in practice

On one view, embedding a link in a website to a third party's site is no different from listing a website address, phone number or mailing address in a printed publication. Since linking is a fundamental part of the World Wide Web, many Internet users assume such links are permitted and some web enthusiasts positively endorse an absolute freedom to link web pages, arguing, with some merit, that this ability is one of the more important things that makes the web such a useful medium. However, many commentators argue that there should be no linking to another site without consent. In the case of framing, it is much clearer that consent should be obtained, as the process of framing lends itself more easily to the possibility that the framer is making a misrepresentation which could be prevented by a passing off or trade mark infringement action.

In practice, it is generally accepted that it is good 'netiquette' to obtain prior approval before linking to an unrelated website, particularly if your website derives income from the links or deprives the target site of advertising income.

In addition, it may not be enough simply to obtain permission to link to third-party sites. Third-party trade marks are often used as the 'link'. Trade mark protection is not limited to mere words and can extend to (amongst other things) logos, colour combinations, fonts, images or even sounds. It is possible therefore that the highlighted text or logo that is included in a site to facilitate a link may in fact be an unauthorised use of a third-party trade mark (for example, use of a hypertext link which is accessed by clicking on the words 'COCA-COLA', together with an icon of the Coca-Cola bottle).

The lesson to be drawn from the recent cases is that the issue is not yet settled and permission should always be sought as to whether and how you propose to link your site to that of a third party.

Notes

1. The right to make copies for back-up or archival purposes is enshrined in section 50A of the Copyright, Designs and Patents Act 1988 (as amended) following the EC Directive on the legal protection of computer programs (No. 91/250/EEC).

2. *Marks and Spencer plc and Others v. One in a Million Ltd*, Court of Appeal, 23 July 1998.

3. *Prince plc v. Prince Sportswear Group Inc.* [1998] FSR 21.

4. *Marks and Spencer plc and Others v. One in a Million*, op. cit.

5. *Shetland Times Limited v. Jonathan Wills* [1997] FSR 604.

6. This, in itself, is unusual as headlines are often thought not to be sufficiently 'literary' to constitute a copyright work.

7. No. 97-3055 DDP (CD Cal., 12 April 1997).

8. (1998) 45 USPQ 2d (BNA) 2005.

CHAPTER 7

Taxation

Background

With e-commerce, a computer user with a modem and the appropriate software can pull onto the information superhighway to locate and access information presented in various forms. The user can then transact business in a number of different ways – for example, ordering goods from on-line catalogues and directories or downloading information from a research database for which payment can be made through the use of electronic payment systems. This chapter looks at the implications and consequences of such commerce in the field of taxation and considers whether existing taxation principles and current tax laws are sufficient to cope with this new type of business.

The tax issues

The real difficulty in taxing e-commerce transactions is how to apply existing tax laws and principles to activities carried out on the Internet. So difficult is this that the OECD instituted two significant conferences to consider the problem. Both the Ottawa and Turku conferences came to the conclusion that the member governments had to provide a fiscal climate within which e-commerce could flourish, weighed against collecting the right amount of tax. The UK government and Inland Revenue participated in both conferences and in October 1998 the Inland Revenue and HM Customs & Excise issued a joint paper on the UK tax policy regarding e-commerce. The UK government recognises the five key principles set out by the OECD:

- *Neutrality* – Taxation should be neutral as between e-commerce and conventional forms of commerce so that neither should be disadvantaged. Taxpayers in similar situations carrying out similar transactions should be subject to similar levels of taxation. There should be no new taxes for e-commerce.

- *Efficiency* – Compliance for taxpayers and administrative costs for the tax authorities should be minimised.

- *Certainty and simplicity* – The tax rules should be clear and simple so that businesses can anticipate the tax consequences in advance of a transaction, including knowing when, where and how the tax is to be accounted for.

- *Effectiveness and fairness* – The tax rules should not result in double taxation or unintentional non-taxation, and risks from increased evasion and avoidance should be kept to a minimum. This is an important area for the various tax administrations because it will become increasingly difficult for them to obtain reliable identification of a taxpayer engaged in e-commerce. For example, it may be impossible to identify the owner of a website conducting trade on the Internet, particularly where the server is located offshore. A website provides no information about the actual owner or where the server is located. In addition, it is very easy to conduct business on the Internet leaving no audit trail, particularly with the increasing use of so-called 'e-cash'. Even if a trail could be found, the increasing availability and complexity of encryption techniques mean transaction details can be hidden from the authorities.

- *Flexibility* – The systems for taxation should be flexible and dynamic so as to keep pace with technological and commercial developments.

The UK government does not believe that at the moment it is necessary to make any major changes to existing tax legislation or regulations or to introduce any new taxes. This means that existing tax principles and legislation will have to be used to deal with e-commerce transactions. In some senses this is unsatisfactory and smacks of trying to fit a quart into a pint pot. In fact, this same attitude was previously adopted by the UK government a decade ago in trying to apply old and long-established tax principles in the field of securities and financial instruments. It became clear very quickly that such principles and existing legislation could not cope with complex financial instruments and derivative transactions. A number of such transactions escaped the UK tax net altogether and led to the total overhaul of the legislation relating to foreign exchange instruments (Finance Act 1993), interest and currency contracts (Finance Act 1994) and loan relationships (Finance Act 1996).

Direct tax aspects

It is necessary, initially, to divide up the tax issues into direct and indirect tax matters. On the direct tax front, two basic concepts underlie a country's ability to tax: residence and source. Residence, because that will be the jurisdiction in which the taxpayer has the closest links; and source, because that is the jurisdiction with which income is most closely connected.

If we look at the UK, for example, the UK levies tax on the world-wide (that is, UK and foreign) income of UK residents, and the UK-source income of non-UK residents. Non-residents will be liable to corporation tax on UK-source income if they carry on a trade through a branch or agency located in the UK, or they may be subject to income tax on UK-source income of a trade within the UK. However, these rules of UK tax law are modified and refined by a number of bilateral double tax treaties entered into by the UK with other jurisdictions. These prevent double taxation by restricting the taxability of source income of non-residents. The concept of a permanent establishment features in all the tax treaties. This basic concept, enshrined in Article 5 of the OECD Model Convention, operates so that if a taxpayer resident in country A (the residence country) has a permanent establishment in country B (the source country), then all of the taxpayer's business profits connected with that permanent establishment may be taxed by country B. If so, those profits will either be exempted from the tax paid in country A or a credit for tax in country B will be given. Where a tax treaty follows the OECD model, in the absence of a permanent establishment, country B cannot tax the taxpayer's profits although it could impose a withholding tax on certain types of income.

If there is a permanent establishment in the UK, then the normal UK rules for taxation of non-residents apply. One must consider whether the permanent establishment also constitutes a branch or agency. Traditionally, only the profits from trade within the UK rather than with the UK have been taxed. The case law is old and mainly involves trade in tangible goods but suggests that contracts formed in the UK will be taxed, whilst those formed outside the UK will not. However, there is a school of thought suggesting that a new line of authority may develop from Atkin LJ's test from *FL Smith & Co v. Greenwood*: 'Where do the operations take place from which the profits in substance arise?'[1] This may be increasingly used since the place of contractual formation test is easily manipulated. Clarification of the issues is necessary but, until then, it is vital that website designers include terms specifying when and where the contract is formed. Note, however, that such terms may not be conclusive.

Applying these principles to e-commerce, it becomes clear that there are two key issues:

- What is a permanent establishment?

- How can one characterise income and payments for e-commerce services?

What is a permanent establishment?

The OECD Model Treaty defines a permanent establishment as:

> *a fixed place of business through which the business of an enterprise is wholly or partly carried on.*

The place of business must therefore have a degree of permanency and a physical presence but does not necessarily have to have a human presence. The commentary to the OECD Model Treaty states that a permanent establishment may exist if the business of an enterprise is carried on mainly through automatic equipment with the activities of personnel restricted to setting up, operating, maintaining and controlling such equipment. An example of this in a recent case is an oil pipeline.[2] But how does this apply to the Internet? Let us take a typical transaction:

> *Mr Watson logs on to his computer in London, dials his ISP which provides a local point of presence. Having verified Mr Watson's identity, he is allowed access to the Internet through his browser software.*

Mr Watson then searches the Internet using one of the search engines such as Yahoo! and finds the retailer that he is looking for, French Music SA. The browser connects Mr Watson to French Music's web server, also located in London, and he views its site. The website permits Mr Watson to place an order for CDs which will be delivered physically by post within 24 hours. Mr Watson orders three CDs and completes the order by entering details of his credit card. In addition, Mr Watson notices that French Music SA also offers a software package 'Cataloguing Your Favourite French Songs', which he decides to buy. Rather than have the CD-ROM delivered manually, he decides to download the software package from the Internet directly onto his personal computer, again paying the fee with his credit card.

This transaction reveals a number of difficult tax questions, among them:

- Can French Music's home page itself, which is accessed by UK customers, constitute a permanent establishment in the UK (whether or not the server was located in or outside the UK)?

- Can the server, located in the UK and used by French Music for its home page, and which can take and fulfil orders, constitute a permanent establishment as French Music in the UK?

The first question is relatively straightforward. A website or web page itself does not constitute a permanent establishment. It is similar to a display of goods or advertising and, under the OECD Model Treaty, this does not constitute a permanent establishment. This is so even if the home page allows the placing and accepting of orders.

A much more difficult question to answer is whether the server constitutes a permanent establishment and this depends on a number of factors. In the present case, the server is located in the UK and, we assume, maintained there by French Music. It is capable of accepting and fulfilling orders. In this case, therefore, the server goes beyond the function of merely soliciting business. It is actually a 'smart' server, carrying out the business. In these circumstances, there is some commentary (including that from the assistant director of the UK Inland Revenue's international division) which suggests that it is sufficient to constitute a permanent establishment through which the business of French Music is carried on. Even with a permanent establishment in the UK, French Music would have to carry on a trade *within* the UK to be liable to UK tax. The contract with UK customers would probably have to be formed in the UK. From a contractual perspective, it throws up an interesting question as to where the contract is concluded. The likely answer, where such 'smart software' is involved, is the UK, because that is the place where notification of the acceptance is received.

In practice, however, is this really likely to occur? Either French Music will operate through a server located outside the UK (and it is interesting to note the growth in companies in Jersey offering server facilities) or it will operate through a leased server on a computer which is owned by an independent third party in the UK. An independent third party will not generally constitute an agency for the purposes of creating a permanent establishment. The current OECD draft on adapting the permanent establishment concept does not defeat this approach. Thus it seems that leasing space on third parties' servers in the UK means there will be no permanent establishment. Alternatively, even where a server is owned in the UK, it is relatively easy to establish an additional server outside the UK (for example, a tax haven) which concludes the contracts with customers. Indeed, it is the very ease with which servers may be leased in jurisdictions with suitable telecommunications infrastructure that may persuade the OECD that servers should not, without fulfilling further requirements, constitute permanent establishments.

The position is further complicated by:

- *Web caching* – Some ISPs serve popular sites on their own computers and thus their customers will be accessing the ISP's computers, not the supplier's server.

- *Mirror sites* – A site to which another website or a set of files can be transferred in order to reduce network traffic or increase access speed. A mirror site is an exact replica of an original site.

- *Smart agents* – The customer may download programs from the supplier's website which perform much of the processing of the customer's order.

The government recently published a paper entitled 'Electronic Commerce: The UK's Taxation Agenda'.[3] It recognised that on the direct tax front, the focus of future work is the OECD and new guidelines are expected on permanent establishments and transfer pricing. It seems likely that the UK taxation authorities will delay issuing general guidance until the OECD has finalised its conclusions. In the meantime, the authorities have indicated that they will offer advice on specific ventures.

If significant amounts of business are relocated to low-taxation jurisdictions, then the Controlled Foreign Companies legislation and transfer pricing legislation will assume increased importance. The UK transfer pricing regime under section 770 of the Income and Corporation Taxes Act 1988 closely follows the OECD model. It essentially means that the amount subject to tax on a transaction between associated parties, where one party is outside the UK charge to tax, will be deemed on an arm's-length basis. This will be relevant if UK entities intend to trade through companies in offshore jurisdictions. If the offshore e-commerce company is simply a distributorship, then these provisions will attribute a low profit margin to such a business and the UK company would be taxed on the majority of the profits. However, the risks and economics of e-commerce are not yet well understood, and so the establishment of arm's-length prices may be difficult.

Characterisation of payments

A second area of concern relates to determining the treatment of payments made under e-commerce. The reason it is important is that if such a payment takes place across borders, then withholding taxes may apply at source on certain types of income (particularly royalties). In many jurisdictions, withholding tax will be relevant to royalty payments for intellectual property or licence fees for the use of computer software under the domestic law of the jurisdiction of the payer. In the UK, for example, payments for the use of or the right to use copyright attract a withholding tax if the owner is not UK-resident. The UK's rules were developed in relation to physical products and it will become increasingly difficult to apply the rules to products which are transmitted electronically. For example, if a consumer makes a payment to download some software which he then uses or perhaps modifies and incorporates into a product which he then sells, is that an acquisition of goods or the payment for copyright? In Mr Watson's case, would the payment for downloading the catalogue software be a payment in the form of a copyright royalty? The sale of shrink-wrapped software to personal customers is generally treated as an absolute sale, whether the software is purchased on, for example, a CD-ROM, or downloaded. The analogy often made is to the sale of a book, which is an absolute sale, but the purchaser is still restricted by copyright in various ways. Where the user is granted rights 'to use the programme in a manner that would, without such licence, constitute an infringement of copyright', the OECD commentary on the Model Convention treats payments for the licence as royalties.

The Internet and indirect taxes

The United States passed the Internet Tax Freedom Act in 1998, which was designed to prevent taxation stifling the growth of the Internet. In relation to US state and local sales taxes, it confirmed that Internet-based contracts do not equate to a sufficient presence for out-of-state vendors to be liable for sales taxes. This approach provides an interesting contrast to that of the European Commission, where the approach seems to be to apply and modify VAT principles to e-commerce to prevent any loss of revenue.

The OECD has focused less on the field of indirect taxation and there is perceived to be an increased risk of double or non-taxation in this area. The primary conclusions of the Ottawa Conference were that:

• consumption taxes should only apply in the jurisdiction of consumption

• supplies of digital products are to be treated as supplies of services.

Value added tax (VAT) is a European Union consumption tax. It is levied on taxable supplies of goods or services made in the European Union by a taxable person in the course or furtherance of any business carried on by him. In general terms, the rules regarding the basis of the charge to VAT are the same across the

EU, although rates of VAT do differ significantly. Goods and services supplied by or through an Internet transaction will attract VAT in the normal way as if they had been supplied by any other means. Indeed, UK Customs & Excise and the European Commission have stated that in this area no new taxes are required. VAT may, however, be adapted to cope with these types of transactions. The question as to whether VAT will therefore apply to an Internet transaction will depend on:

- the nature of the supply

- the place of supply

- the nature and location of the supplier

- the type of consumer.

The place of supply determines whether any VAT is payable, that is, if outside the EU then no VAT will be charged on the supply. However, the rules that decide where the supply is made depend on whether the supply is of goods or services. In the context of Internet transactions, there are three broad types of transaction:

1   the ordering of goods on-line where the goods are then physically delivered (that is, the Internet is akin to a mail-order catalogue), which is currently the most common type of transaction

2   the supply of digitised products from one business to another business where the property is supplied through the Internet (for example, downloading software onto the customer's own terminal) – often known as 'the supply of digitised products'

3   the supply of services of the same type as in 2 above.

Ordering goods

The supply of products which are physically delivered will be treated as a supply of goods. Accordingly the normal rules for the supply of goods apply, namely:

- *sale within a member state (say the UK)* – VAT is chargeable in that member state

- *goods sent to a business consumer in another member state of the EU* – no UK VAT but the customer will operate the reverse charge procedure and account for VAT in its own jurisdiction

- *goods sent to a private consumer in another EU state* – UK VAT chargeable

- *goods sent outside the EU* – no UK VAT chargeable (in some cases the supplier will have to register and account for VAT in that other state)

- *goods imported into the UK from outside the EU* – UK VAT payable on import on the value of the goods for customs duty.

The EU is considering improved procedures for the anticipated increase in imported goods as a result of the increase in e-commerce. Other than that, since the goods are still physically delivered, the mere fact that they were ordered electronically gives rise to no significant new problems.

The supply of services

The supply of on-line services and digitised products is now generally treated as a supply of services (in most member states being treated as a supply of information). On basic principles, services consumed in the EU should be taxed in the EU. This treatment may show up some anomalies in the rates of tax applied to tangible and digitised products – for instance, books are zero-rated in the UK but in digitised form the product is a supply of information services and standard-rated. (Note that this directly contravenes the principle of neutrality discussed above.) However, the greater and more persistent problems in this area are found, as with direct tax, in determining the place of supply (where the product should be taxed with VAT) when such products are supplied across national borders.

The place of supply of services is generally the place where the supplier belongs, and 'belonging' for this purpose means the place where the supplier has a business or other fixed establishment. This could bring one back to the question of whether a website or server can constitute an establishment. However, as supplies of information services or copyright, almost all digitised products are deemed to be supplied where received if the customer is either outside the EU or is a business in the EU (see Article 9(2)(e) of the Sixth Directive).[4] The problems can therefore be resolved with business consumers but are much more difficult where private consumers in the EU are concerned.

- *Business consumers* – In the case of a supply of on-line services or digitised products to a business in a member state, the accepted mechanism for collecting VAT on international supplies is the reverse charge procedure under Article 9(2)(e) of the Sixth Directive. The business consumer will account to his own revenue authority for VAT, that is, in the place where the service is consumed, and the supplier is not required to pay the tax in its own member state.

- *Private consumers* – Private consumers could not be expected to operate the reverse charge procedure and indeed by definition cannot be held liable for the tax under the Sixth Directive. The supplier of the services must therefore account for the VAT. If the supplier is a business in another member state, that is where he must account for VAT on all supplies to private customers in his own or another state. If the supplier is outside the member states and has no place of business in the EU, the only alternative is to require him to account for the tax in the place of consumption, either directly or through a fiscal representative.

In the context of the provision of telecommunication and Internet services, non-EU-based providers used to have an advantage over EU-based providers in that they would not charge VAT to private consumers on the supply of certain telecommunication services, including call back and mobile phone services. However, this has been remedied by applying Article 9(3)(b) of the Sixth Directive, which states that the place of supply will be where the use and enjoyment of the service takes place. Consequently, the overseas entity providing the service is effectively required to register in the relevant EU state.

The same approach could be taken for the supply of digitised products and services on the Internet, but there would need to be additional safeguards to ensure compliance and, until that happens, UK Customs & Excise will decline to apply Article 9(3)(b) of the Directive. Some member states, including France and Italy, have decided to apply Article 9(3)(b). In the UK therefore currently, a supplier of on-line Internet services based in and acting from the United States providing services such as music software which UK consumers can download will not have to charge VAT. A UK competitor would. Moreover, VAT paid by EU exporters of services to EU private customers is paid in the exporting country at the rate prevailing in that country. This is contrary to the OECD vision that consumption taxes should be paid in the country of consumption and may lead to VAT rates (at least for these services) converging.

The provision of services to private consumers is the key issue for the future. Clearly, tax must be accounted for where the service is consumed but this raises issues of enforcement. A consensus is needed amongst the major nations as to how to identify and report transactions and how to collect tax on these transactions. A number of suggestions have been made: that businesses with websites should display their VAT registration; that one registration within the EU will suffice; and that ISPs and operators of payment systems should have reporting and accounting obligations placed on them. These issues are being considered by the OECD's fiscal affairs committee. Its report will make interesting reading.

In the meantime, the European Commission issued a working paper on indirect taxes and e-commerce on 8 June 1999. It reiterates the Commission's determination that e-commerce should be properly covered by the VAT system. The paper confirms that electronic deliveries should be treated as supplies of services and taxed in the jurisdiction of consumption. The Commissioners have rejected self-assessment for VAT by consumers and withholding taxes collected by banks or payment systems. Instead, the paper contains proposals for registration requirements for non-EU service providers. The other big issue, that of how to identify customers as business or final consumers, is also addressed.

Finally, it is proposed that the place-of-supply rules of Article 9 should be changed. There are relatively few internationally traded services outside the reverse charge rules of Article 9(2)(e). It is proposed that this should be extended to all services supplied from outside the EU for consumption by businesses within the EU. Service providers based outside the EU would have to register and account for VAT on supplies to private consumers. These changes would go well beyond those necessary for e-commerce. However, they require unanimous consent from the Council of Ministers before they can be implemented and this could take some time.

The way forward

There are still many uncertainties in this area, some of which should be dispelled by the various OECD reports and the government's response. However, until these have bedded down, specialist tax advice will often be necessary.

Notes

1. (1922) 8TC 193.

2. Bundesfinanzhof 30 October 1996.

3. <www.inlandrevenue.gov.uk/e-commerce/ecom3.htm>.

4. Sixth Council Directive 77/388/EEC (as amended) OJ L 145 13/6/77.

CHAPTER 8

....

Electronic signatures and the security of electronic transactions

Encryption

Encryption is at the heart of electronic commerce. The fact that the technologies underpinning the Internet were initially developed not with secrecy in mind but to ensure the operational integrity of the networks has meant that communications carried out over the Internet are perceived by some as being essentially open to eavesdropping. The truth is somewhat different but, to counter this openness and provide for some degree of confidentiality, encryption tools have nevertheless been developed for use across the Internet.

Encryption technology does not just provide for secrecy or confidentiality. The greatest interest from a commercial standpoint is its ability to provide the technology needed to create and validate electronic signatures. Electronic commerce, unlike other forms of commerce, is completely blind in that both parties may not have any satisfactory means of verifying the other's identity (that is, the authenticity of the message sent) or that the message has not been tampered with (that is, the integrity of the message). Encryption allows them to verify each other's identity and to guarantee the integrity of the data flow to a high degree of certainty.

While governments are very keen to promote e-commerce, those same governments often attempt to control or restrict the use of encryption technology. Ironically, however, though there is very little control over the use of encryption within the United States and Canada, the US government was perhaps the most vociferous when it came to controlling the export of encryption technology. The UK government has itself been toying with the idea of strong encryption control. However, the reaction to the proposed controls in the UK was such that when the UK government finally published the Electronic Communications Bill (to the day, one year after the European Commission first published its proposed E-Commerce Directive), the measures that were initially under consideration – that is, to require Internet service providers to place encryption keys in escrow for government agency use in certain circumstances ('key escrow') – were omitted. Unfortunately, the Bill still contained encryption-related provisions that were less than helpful and it seems the matter of encryption control will be revisited when the UK government comes to amending its Interception of Communications Act 1985.

The US government seems to have recognised the difficulty that its computer security industry faced as a result of the restrictions on the export of encryption technology in the International Traffic in Arms Regulations and the Export Administration Regulations. On 6 September 1999, the White House announced that those regulations governing the export of non-military encryption technology would be relaxed. The new regulations were published in interim form in the Federal Register on 14 January 2000 and will be reviewed again prior to publishing the regulations in their final form. One of the key reasons the regulations were amended was to create a more liberal licensing regime as a direct result of developments in other jurisdictions.

Electronic signatures

Encryption technologies provide the ability to create and validate electronic signatures through the use of what is called 'asynchronous' or 'public key' cryptography. This essentially uses two keys to encrypt and decrypt messages. A message encrypted with one key can only be decrypted with the other key. It is this feature that is used for signatures. Using this technique, a person will 'sign' a document with their private key. Anyone can then use the corresponding public key to verify the identity of the signatory, as only their private key will correspond. That is the theory. In practice, there still needs to be some way of identifying the owner or holder of the private key and verifying that identity. It is here that the so-called 'trusted third parties' come into play.

Trusted third parties

Essentially, the role of a trusted third party is to identify the owner or holder of a signature, although this role could be extended to encompass key generation, key escrow or other related functions (including the provision of cryptography services such as the provision of an encrypted messaging service and the archiving and retrieval of electronic data). At its simplest, the trusted third party would certify that to the best of its knowledge the identity of the signature holder is that which is claimed. This cannot be absolutely certain, just as, in the non-digital world, identity cannot always be absolutely certain. Certificates of identity given by the trusted third party can operate in many ways, from being incorporated into the signature itself, through to independent verification of the public key.

Key escrow is championed by national authorities, including law enforcement agencies, and involves an authority or a trusted third party holding a copy of the key in escrow to be used for the prevention or detection of serious crime. The private sector has concerns about public access to private data, albeit such access would be regulated. As indicated above, the UK government seems to have dropped its plans for key escrow at present, though it seems likely that some form of access controls will be imposed when it presents its proposed amendments to the current law which is set out in the Interception of Communications Act 1985 as contained in the Regulation of Investigatory Powers Bill.

Contractual requirements

Electronic signatures are feasible and they can perform the function of identifying a party or person. But will that function be enough to satisfy the requirements of the law? Electronic signatures have a great many uses, from acting as electronic 'watermarks' and time/date stamps, through to acting as electronic surrogates for signatures in electronic contracts. The most troublesome use is the latter. For an electronic signature to be valid in an electronic contract, and this only if such a contract may be entered into in the first instance, it must satisfy the requirements of a signature in the 'normal' form of the contract. Where the signature simply identifies the parties to the contract, such as with an arm's-length business-to-business non-regulated transaction, this is not usually a problem. Problems start to occur where legal and regulatory requirements dictate that the contract must be 'in writing signed by the parties' or where the signature must be 'in writing' or where it requires there to be a 'mark' on the document. In these circumstances (which are common in the laws relating to testamentary dispositions or the assignment of real or intellectual property), an electronic signature would almost certainly fail to satisfy these requirements.

Both the UK government and the European Commission have recognised that statutory requirements requiring documents to be 'in writing' or 'signed' are significant barriers to the development of electronic commerce. The recently adopted Electronic Signatures Directive[1] addresses this issue by requiring member states to give legal force to electronic signatures which satisfy certain requirements (which are technology-neutral). However, the UK's recently published Electronic Communications Bill does not address this issue directly. Instead, it provides that an electronic signature and its certification should be admissible in evidence as to the authenticity and integrity of an electronic communication. 'Electronic signature' is defined broadly and the UK government has left it open to courts to decide whether an electronic signature has been correctly used and has evidential weight. Therefore, although the DTI has said that the Electronic Communications Bill implements the EC Electronic Signatures Directive, this is debatable. In addition, the Bill enables ministers to draw up secondary legislation to facilitate the general use of electronic communications or storage. Again, this section is so broadly drafted that its meaning is difficult to ascertain. It remains to be seen to what extent such powers would be used and when – and indeed whether – these provisions will survive the process of parliamentary scrutiny.

European regulatory initiatives

In December 1999, the European Commission adopted the Electronic Signatures Directive as a response to the development of legislation by individual member states. In addition to the requirement on member states to provide for the legal recognition of electronic signatures, the main thrust of the legislation is that of mutual recognition – that is, member states must recognise the validity of certificates that originate from trusted third parties in other member states. This may seem of little consequence but it will have a profound effect. The proposal does not mandate licensing for trusted third parties; that is left for the member states to decide for themselves (the UK appears to have decided on a non-mandatory approval scheme in the Electronic Communications Bill). The proposal would, however, enable users to obtain certificates from any trusted third party in the EU and then use that certificate with the knowledge that it will be accepted throughout the EU. In short, users will be free to choose where they obtain their certificates, keys or other services. The Directive also requires the trusted third parties to be liable for loss caused by their negligence in issuing certificates. The Electronic Signatures Directive must be implemented by 19 July 2001.

Note

1. Directive 1999/93/EC of the European Parliament and the Council of 13 December 1999 on a Community framework for electronic signatures.

CHAPTER 9

Advertising and marketing

Global advertising

General

Advertising often appears on websites. Indeed, websites themselves which may be accessed around the world are a form of advertising and marketing. However, genuine global advertising campaigns are rare. Many considerations dictate advertising and marketing initiatives used in different countries, whether they be cultural, linguistic or legal.

In the developed world, the advertising of some products or services tends to be more heavily regulated than others – for example, financial services, pharmaceutical products, gambling and adult services are all subject to a raft of statutory and non-statutory rules and codes of practice. We focus on the financial services sector in more detail in the next chapter, but special attention should be given to the rules and regulations that will apply to other sectors. See, for example, the report prepared by Ashurst Morris Crisp for the European Commission, 'The Impact of E-Commerce on the European Pharmaceutical Sector'.[1]

Given any advertisement on the Internet can potentially be viewed anywhere in the world, do advertisers and marketers need to consider the advertising laws of every jurisdiction? Advertising which is lawful or not heavily regulated in one country may not be lawful, or may be heavily regulated, in another. Legal consequences such as product liability and rules with respect to comparative advertising may be more severe in some countries than in others. Yet clearing the advertising and marketing material used on the Internet in order to ensure compliance with every single legal system is a task which is complicated, time-consuming and expensive – and virtually impossible.

What can be done?

As with trade marks, it is important at least to identify the key territories where you intend to carry on significant business, as well as those territories where advertising is heavily regulated. Clearances should then be sought in these countries.

Further, disclaimers or explanatory text should be used to indicate which markets you intend to target (for example, you could specify that you do not do business in certain territories). As discussed previously, it is still an open question as to whether a UK court would uphold such disclaimers. However, it is advisable to include them.

Product liability

Websites often provide descriptions of the products for sale, including claims about those products, which may be untrue or misleading or form the basis of or assist product liability claims (whether in misrepresentation, negligence or breach of contract). On-line suppliers will typically seek to exclude or restrict such liability, again through use of appropriately worded disclaimers. Under English law, such exclusions or restrictions may in many cases be subject to the requirements of the Unfair Contract Terms Act 1977 and, if so, will be subject to review as to their enforceability – some will be unenforceable *per se*, others will only be enforceable if reasonable. Similar consumer protection laws operate in other jurisdictions.

Advertising in the UK

Advertising law in the UK stems both from legislation which impacts upon advertising and industry codes of conduct.

Of particular relevance are the British Codes of Advertising and Sales Promotion (Codes) whose requirements are policed by the Advertising Standards Authority. The Codes contain general principles covering all advertisements, as well as specific rules dealing with particular products, such as tobacco, alcoholic drinks and advertisements aimed at children. Their basic tenet is that all advertisements should be legal, decent, honest and truthful. However, it is not entirely clear as to whether the Codes regulate Internet-related activities. They are expressed to apply to what is known as 'viewdata' services but do not apply to 'broadcast commercials' or 'advertisements in foreign media'.

A number of statutes in the UK also impact upon advertising on the Internet. For example, the Trade Descriptions Act 1968 makes it a criminal offence to apply a false trade description to goods. The Control of Misleading Advertisements Regulations 1988 enables the Director General of the Office of Fair Trading to control advertisements which 'deceive or are likely to deceive'.

It has also been argued that the existing body of broadcasting legislation may apply to advertising on the Internet to the extent that the Internet can be regarded as a 'broadcast'. Some commentators believe that those carrying out marketing and advertising activities via the Internet may be forced to obtain a licence under the Broadcasting Act 1990, with the material in that broadcast being subject to the Independent Television Commission codes (for example, the ITC Code of Advertising Standards and Practice and the ITC Rules and Advertising Rates).

Finally, sales promotion schemes, including free prize draws and prize competitions, are regulated in the UK under the Lotteries and Amusements Act 1976. The peculiarities of the Internet must be taken into account with on-line promotional offers. When running a competition on a website, it may be worth considering restricting eligibility for entry to residents of countries where legal clearances have been obtained.

The proposed Electronic Commerce Directive

Impact on advertising and marketing

On 18 November 1998, a proposal for a Directive was issued by the European Commission (amended in May 1999) dealing with 'certain aspects of electronic commerce in the internal market'. Many of its provisions have been criticised.

The proposal applies to those who supply and receive 'information society services', which are defined as those 'normally provided for remuneration, at a distance, by electronic means at the individual request of a recipient of services'.

This broad definition spans a wide range of economic activities, including on-line selling of goods, newspapers, financial services, marketing and advertising and even professional services. It contemplates both business-to-business and business-to-consumer services, including services provided free of charge to recipients (for example, where funded by advertising or sponsorship revenue or revenue generated from the use of the transmission networks).

In particular, the proposed Directive purports to regulate 'commercial communications', which are defined as any form of communication designed to promote (directly or indirectly) the goods, services or image of a company, person or organisation. This wide definition would therefore include promotional offers (such as discounts or gifts), advertising and promotional competitions. However, it does not include the mere ownership of a website, provision of information which is not promotional, or the mere mention of a domain name, email address, logo or brand name where there is no financial nexus to its proprietor (that is, independent promotion). Gambling is specifically excluded although some commentators have pointed out that it will be difficult to determine in some circumstances whether a competition with financial prizes is indeed a competition or 'gambling'.

What about 'spam'?

Direct marketing organisations have been quick to seize upon the opportunity that the Internet affords by using the medium to market directly to many ISP subscribers. The process of sending unsolicited email to consumers or discussion groups, otherwise known as 'spamming', has become widespread and has been the subject of litigation in the US courts (for example, in *CompuServe Inc. v. Cyber Promotions*[2] it was held that spamming constituted trespass). The UK courts have yet to address this issue (although, in at least one case which settled, trespass claims were made by the Internet service provider, Virgin Net).

The proposed Directive deals with spamming to a limited extent. Accordingly, to permit recipients of spam to react more readily to harmful intrusion, the proposed Directive requires these emails to have a specific message on their envelopes to enable their recipient to identify them as spam without having to open them. Unfortunately, the proposal gives no clear guidance as to how this identification should be achieved. However, member states will be required to ensure that consumers can avoid such unwanted correspondence by entering their names on an 'opt out' register. Member states will also be required to impose legal requirements on suppliers to inform customers of their data protection rights (see Chapter 11).

Marketing organisations have criticised the provisions, arguing that direct marketers will be penalised in electronic marketing where they are not in more traditional forms of marketing. Conversely, email activists have warned that while the present proposal requires spam to be identified as such, there is no provision to stop companies sending unsolicited mail in the first place. It remains to be seen how the European Commission proposes to deal with the concerns of these groups.

Notes

1. Available to be downloaded at <www.ashursts.com>.

2. No. C2-96-1070 (SD Oh., 3 February 1997).

CHAPTER 10

· ·

Financial services and the Internet

Apart from issues relating to security (discussed in Chapter 8), there are two key areas which are particular to the marketing of investments and financial services on the Internet. First, there are a number of restrictions on the advertising of financial services and investments. Second, businesses that want to offer financial services via the Internet, or to link up with financial services providers by providing Internet services, need to consider what restrictions there are on the conduct of their business and what authorisations are required from the authorities in the countries in which they plan to do business. Each of these key areas must be considered, of course, in the context of the global reach of the Internet.

Advertising financial services on the Internet

For financial services providers, like all other businesses, the root of the problem lies in the fact that, though it is possible for someone anywhere in the world to access financial information posted on a website, nearly every jurisdiction has its own laws regarding the advertising or provision of financial services in its territory. Potentially, therefore, the issuer of an advertisement on the Internet could breach the laws of over a hundred jurisdictions with a single advert. This situation may arise even though the advertisement is only directed at the issuer's home market or at a few selected territories. Clearly, therefore, any analysis of, and response to, this problem has to be truly global in nature, and to involve the governments and regulators of many countries. It is encouraging to note that international initiatives are under way, principally through IOSCO (the International Organisation of Securities Commissions), though there is presently some way to go. These international initiatives are discussed below.

The UK position

At present, UK financial services are governed by various statutes, including the Financial Services Act 1986 (the 1986 Act). The 1986 Act was not drafted with e-commerce in mind and, as a result, the concepts used in the 1986 Act are very hard to fit into the context of the electronic marketplace.

The 1986 Act makes it a criminal offence to issue an 'investment advertisement' unless the advertisement is issued or approved by a UK authorised person or a European investment firm (for example, an authorised French investment bank or German broker/dealer), subject to any available exemption. There are a few exemptions which are frequently relied on where the intended recipients of an advertisement are, for example, professionals or persons presumed to have knowledge of the service or investment being marketed. It is self-evident, though, that these may be difficult to rely on in the context of the Internet, especially if the issuer of an advertisement has no control over the people who can access and read it.

The definition of an 'investment advertisement' in section 57(2) of the 1986 Act is very wide. Any advertisement containing information which is likely to lead to a person entering into an investment agreement will, *prima facie*, be an investment advertisement.

To be caught by UK regulation, however, an advertisement must be *issued* in the UK. The question arises whether the mere availability of an advertisement on an overseas website will result in the issue of that advertisement in the UK. The UK's Financial Services Authority, or FSA, thinks that it will:

> *Where information held anywhere on the Net is made available to or can be obtained by someone in the UK that information, if it takes the form of an investment advertisement, may be viewed as having been issued in the UK.*[1]

This looks worrying for Internet advertisers of financial services and, in fairness to the UK regulators, a similar view is taken by various other regulators world-wide on the basis of their respective laws. The FSA has, however, given helpful guidance on the factors which it will take into account when deciding on the enforcement action to be taken in relation to 'unapproved' investment advertisements. These factors include the following:

- whether the website was located on a server outside the UK

- whether the investment or service was available to UK investors who may respond

- whether positive steps have been taken to limit access to the site (for example, pre-registration, passwords)

- whether positive steps have been taken to avoid UK investors accepting the investment/service (for example, requirements to provide personal information, including information on country of origin)

- the extent to which the advertisement was *directed towards* the UK

- the potential risks to UK investors

- other potential infringements of UK law in respect of the website.

None of these factors alone is conclusive, but the question of whether the advertisement is *directed towards* the UK is particularly important. Evidence that the site may, or may not, be directed at UK investors may include:

- disclaimers/warnings regarding the availability of services in certain countries. These warnings may be found on home pages or application pages, or through hypertext links from these pages to other pages

- notification to a UK search engine or a UK compendium of websites

- the existence of other e-facilities linked to the site promoting UK investment (for example, bulletin boards, chatrooms, email)

- the existence of other advertising (for example, newspapers, periodicals, mailshots).

The 1986 Act is due to be replaced in early 2000 by the new Financial Services and Markets Act, which will replace the law on investment advertising with a new concept of 'financial promotion'. Though the new definitions are not yet entirely clear, the Treasury has already said that the extent to which an advertisement is directed at the UK will be relevant to the question of whether a promotion is caught by UK law and regulation. This would be preferable to the existing position, which relies heavily on the enforcement policy of the FSA itself.

International regulatory response

The international regulatory response is developing along similar lines to those described above. A common approach is evident among many national regulators; this was detailed in 1998 in an Internet Report produced by the International Organisation for Securities Commissions (IOSCO).[2] Broadly, the emerging consensus is that regulatory intervention in relation to the promotion and conduct of financial services should not be triggered by the availability of information to local persons but by financial services being targeted or directed at those persons. A website operator may be able to avoid local regulation if it implements procedures properly designed to prevent access to foreign nationals – for example, through the use of appropriate technology, passwords or warnings. However, in relation to fraud or market manipulation, jurisdiction is generally asserted where it affects the jurisdiction or its investors.

In the United States, the Securities and Exchange Commission (SEC) has published an Interpretative Release (March 1998) on the use of websites which distinguishes between ordinary website postings and targeted Internet communications, such as email. Generally, the SEC considers that if providers take measures on their sites which are reasonably designed to guard against sales to US persons, then the use of their websites will not be deemed to be 'targeted' at US persons and will not require registration under US Securities Registration legislation. The 'reasonable measures' suggested by the SEC for overseas businesses are similar to those suggested by the FSA in the UK, such as disclaimers and warnings and requirements for the investor to provide an address and other personal information.

UK authorisation

At the time of writing, there are different authorisation requirements applying to the banking, insurance and investment industries, though these should be significantly harmonised over the next twelve to eighteen months under the new Financial Services and Markets Bill. However, in terms of marketing and selling, there are presently some financial products – most notably mortgages and general insurance – which may be sold with relatively little formal legal restriction. The UK government has, however, its eye on those areas which are presently unregulated, or less regulated, and this position may change.

In relation to regulated financial services, mainstream financial firms are likely to be well acquainted with their positions in relation to Internet activities (each of the self-regulating organisations – including FSA and IMRO – have published relevant guidance for their members during the past two years).

However, the position of unregulated Internet service or access providers needs careful examination. The FSA published some guidance for Internet access and site providers in 1997 which stated that such persons would not be conducting 'investment business' under the 1986 Act if they merely acted as a conduit through which other persons gained access to information on the Internet and provided they have no knowledge of, or control over, the information or service being provided.

However, many service providers may not be satisfied to be merely 'conduits'. In such cases, the FSA says that service providers may need to be authorised if they are more 'commercially involved' with the service or investment being marketed. Such involvement may include:

- involvement in and/or control over the information placed on the site

- joint venture arrangements with financial service providers

- active promotion of financial services under the access provider's own name or the name of the financial service provider, or

- a financial interest in the service being provided (for example, entitlement to commissions).

You may ask how an Internet service provider could be caught if the financial service or product belongs to the bank or investment firm in question and the Internet service provider does not give advice. The answer is partly that the categories of 'investment business' under the 1986 Act include the category of 'arranging deals in investments' which is particularly broad and includes:

making arrangements with a view to another person who participates in the arrangements buying, selling, subscribing for or underwriting investments.

The scope of this is such that potentially it could capture, for example, the act of providing a hypertext link from a general advertising page to the home page of a financial product provider. Alternatively, listing available PEPs or ISAs in a top-ten order, together with a hyperlink service to the application page for subscription to those PEPs or ISAs, may well constitute the act of arranging deals in investments, particularly if the service justifies the payment of commissions or referral fees to the service provider as part of an arrangement with a financial firm. If this is correct, the arrangements may constitute an authorisable activity and as such a criminal offence if the website provider is not itself authorised or exempted. Interactive sites, where the investor is able to input personal information and obtain investment options, again with hypertext links to financial firms' sites, are also at risk. The FSA is reviewing websites in this respect and, we understand, is presently taking the view that it will first request that a provider which it believes has breached the 1986 Act ceases or changes its site before any formal enforcement action is taken. However, this approach cannot be guaranteed in the future.

It is also possible for a service provider to give investment advice. For example, an interactive service may produce a specific recommendation once the user has input personal information. Also, some sites are, in effect, financial journals which can, in some cases, contain specific recommendations or advice. In the case of such journals, however, authorisation can be avoided in respect of advice given 'if the principal purpose of the publication taken as a whole, and including any advertisements contained in it, is not to lead persons to invest in any particular investment'.

The FSA will, on request, review a website to assess whether it can be certified as an exempt newspaper or journal for these purposes.

Cross-border business

Financial service providers and others also need to consider whether services provided cross-border to persons resident in another country will require either authorisation in that country or, in the case of European investment firms providing services into other member states, compliance with local conduct-of-business requirements. The question of where a particular service is carried out can be complex and will depend on the facts. Interestingly, the European Commission has recommended in relation to banking services that European member states should consider such services to have been provided within their territory only if the essential feature – or characteristic performance – of the services was provided within the territory. The Commission also states that mere advertising, or the provision of distance banking services, through the Internet will not, of itself, amount to the provision of services in the host state. However, one must look at the key characteristics of each service or transaction to decide where it is performed.

Unfortunately, the European Commission's recommendation has not been universally applied by member states, and interested firms should accordingly take advice on a country-by-country basis where appropriate.

Notes

1. SIB Guidance Release, 17 June 1996. (The Securities and Investment Board is now known as the Financial Services Authority.)

2. Securities Activity on the Internet; A Report of the Technical Committee of the International Organisation of Securities Commissions, September 1998. <www.iosco.org/docs-public/1998-internet_security.html>.

CHAPTER 11

● ●

Data protection

The Data Protection Directive

The EU Data Protection Directive[1] aims to harmonise European data protection laws and allow for the free flow of personal data within Europe. The UK has implemented the Directive by the Data Protection Act 1998 (the 1998 Act), which came into force on 1 March 2000. Because of the global nature of the Internet, data controllers may well find that they have to comply with data protection regimes in various countries and it should not be forgotten that existing regimes in some European countries are, in some respects, more stringent than those set out in the Directive.

Since the definition of 'processing' in the Directive is extremely broad, it is difficult to think of any use of personal data on the Internet which will not amount to processing.[2] Therefore thought should be given to compliance with relevant requirements when setting up a website, and in particular a trading website, so that the steps which need to be taken to ensure compliance are built in at an early stage. Although this may seem to be yet another hurdle when looking at e-commerce, the fact that a website owner has focused on this issue can be used to encourage customers to use that website confidently, that is, knowing how their personal data may be used and that their personal data are secure.

The data protection regime in the UK under the Data Protection Act 1998 is based on a structure which broadly consists of:

- notification to the Data Protection Registry by those who use personal data of the types and purposes of processing to which the data will be subject

- compliance with general data protection principles, and

- an independent supervisory body.

The UK Data Protection Act 1998

The 1998 Act applies to a data controller if (i) the data controller is 'established' in the UK and the data are processed in the context of that establishment, or (ii) the data controller is established neither in the UK nor in any other EEA state but uses equipment in the UK for processing the data otherwise than for the purposes of transit through the UK. Those established include:

- an individual who is ordinarily resident in the UK

- a body incorporated under English law

- a partnership or other unincorporated association formed under English law, or

- any person who maintains an office, branch or agency in the UK.

Important definitions in the Act include the following:

- *'Personal data'* means data which relate to a living individual who can be identified from those data, or from those data and other information which is in the possession of, or is likely to come into the possession of, the data controller. Expressions of opinion and indications of intentions of anyone in respect of the individual are also included.

- *'Processing'* is defined extremely broadly and it is likely that any activities carried out in relation to personal data will amount to processing.

- A *'data controller'* is a person who (either alone or jointly or in common with other persons) determines the purposes for which and the manner in which any personal data are, or are to be, processed. Hence an entity setting up an Internet trading site will be the data controller of the personal data processed via that site. However, it is also possible that there may be other data controllers, such as the ISP which hosts the site, if it carries out any processing of the personal data.

- *'Sensitive personal data'* is a new category of personal data and includes personal data consisting of information as to racial or ethnic origin, political opinions, religious beliefs, physical or mental health, or sexual life.

The first data protection principle

There are eight main principles under the Data Protection Act 1998, the first of which is that *processing* be fair and lawful; in order to comply with this, there are various conditions, at least one of which must be met. The most relevant conditions are that the data subject has given his or her consent to the processing, or that the processing is necessary for the performance of a contract to which the data subject is a party. Consent should generally be explicit but can be implied in limited circumstances. Where data are deemed to be *sensitive personal data,* further more stringent conditions apply and explicit consent will generally need to be obtained.

Where the *personal data* are used for non-contractual purposes such as marketing, profiling or advertising, consent will need to be obtained for such processing and information provided about these purposes. Special attention will need to be paid to the use of 'cookies' and other information-gathering technologies.[3]

As well as meeting these conditions, *data controllers* must comply with the Fair Processing Code. Broadly, this code sets out requirements for the fair obtaining of personal data and in particular the information which is to be provided to individuals. This information includes the purposes for which the personal data are intended to be processed, the identity of the data controller and any further information which is required in the circumstances to ensure that the processing is fair. This is in addition to the obligation to notify the Data Protection Registry of the processing which is to be undertaken.[4]

The Data Protection Commissioner has said that, because personal data input on the Internet are immediately capable of being processed, the information required to be given under the Fair Processing Code should be presented before the individual submits any information. This will ensure that the individual can decide, with full information, whether or not to proceed with the transaction and requires that, in the design of a website, data protection rules are taken into account at an early stage.

The eighth data protection principle

The eighth principle prohibits the transfer of personal data to countries outside the European Economic Area which do not have adequate levels of data protection. This prohibition does not apply in certain situations, which include where the data subject has given his or her consent, where the transfer is necessary for the performance of a contract between the data subject and the data controller, and where the transfer is made on terms which have been approved by the Data Protection Commissioner as ensuring adequate protection.

This principle is highly problematic for e-commerce because few countries outside Europe have levels of data protection regulation that are deemed by Europe to be adequate. Website owners have little control over who can access their sites and servers could be located virtually anywhere. In particular, the US is not deemed to have adequate protections and for over two years negotiations continued between the EU and the US as to how the Directive would affect transatlantic data flows. The two sides have recently reached an agreement which essentially provides that the US will establish a safe harbour which will be a voluntary scheme whereby US companies can sign up to a data protection regime. Companies that do sign up to the safe harbour will be deemed to provide adequate protection and therefore transfers of personal data from Europe will not be prohibited by the eighth data protection principle. This proposal needs to be ratified by the various authorities before it comes into effect. For other countries outside the EEA, there are procedures for general findings of adequacy and the UK Data Protection Commissioner has issued preliminary guidance on how to assess whether there are adequate protections so that transfers can take place. It is also likely, now that the US negotiations have concluded, that model contract clauses which could be used for transfers may be approved. However, there are various issues over the adequacy of the protection offered to individuals under such clauses.

Other data protection principles

The remaining data protection principles require that personal data must not be processed in any manner incompatible with the notified purposes, and that the personal data must be relevant and not excessive in relation to the purposes for which those data are processed. Website registration forms may ask for personal data beyond what is necessary and fall foul of these principles. Personal data must also be kept accurate and up to date, and must not be kept for longer than necessary for the stated purpose(s).

Another important principle relates to the security of the personal data against unauthorised processing and against accidental loss of, or damage to, personal data. This principle applies not only to processing carried out by the data controller itself, but also governs how processing can be carried out on behalf of a data controller by a third party. This is important to consider when contracting with ISPs or other parties which may process personal data jointly with, or on behalf of, the data controller.

Rights of data subjects

Rights of individuals have been extended under the 1998 Act. Of particular interest are the right of subject access, the right to prevent processing for the purposes of direct marketing, rights in relation to automated decision-taking, and the right to take action for compensation.

In relation to subject access, data controllers should be aware that generally an individual has a right to be provided with copies of all information held about that individual. Website systems should be structured so that requests can be satisfied as easily as possible, since enormous amounts of personal data are likely to be held – such as, for example, records of all visits made to a site by an individual.

Penalties for non-compliance

The Data Protection Act 1998 gives the Data Protection Commissioner wider enforcement powers than those available under the 1984 Act. Data controllers can be served with enforcement notices requiring them to take various steps or to refrain from processing certain personal data. The 1998 Act also gives the Commissioner wider information-gathering powers in the form of information notices. Failure to comply with these notices or providing false information in respect of a notice is an offence and, where an offence is committed by a company and is proved to have been committed with the consent of, or due to neglect on the part of, an officer of the company or someone purporting to act in that capacity, that person as well as the company will be guilty of an offence. There are provisions for data controllers to appeal to a tribunal against the terms of a notice, as well as provisions for appeals to the High Court on points of law from decisions of the tribunal. The Commissioner can also, with a warrant, enter and search premises, seize documents and other material, and operate and test equipment used for processing.

Offences under the 1998 Act are punishable by fines which can be unlimited. However, as was evidenced in the *British Gas* and the *Midlands Electricity* cases,[5] two of the most significant reasons to ensure compliance are to avoid bad publicity and a prohibition on the use of personal data in breach of the Act.

Conclusion

Data protection is becoming increasingly regulated, both within and outside Europe. The Data Protection Commissioner is concerned about misuse of personal data on the Internet. However, despite the fact that the threat posed by technology was one of the main reasons for the existence of such regulation, the legislation is not well tailored to the Internet, which means that compliance can be onerous. Compliance is made more onerous by the fact that until the courts clarify the meaning of some of the concepts enshrined in the 1998 Act, the advice offered by the Data Protection Commissioner's office is cautious.

Notes

1. Directive 95/46/EC.

2. In *Source Informatics Ltd* (CA) 21 December 1999 (unreported), the court expressed the view that making data anonymous 'was not objectionable under domestic law'. This could be argued to mean that it did not amount to processing within the meaning of the 1998 Act, although the court's reasoning is not at all clear and, on the face of it, it seems impossible to reconcile this view with the definition of processing under the 1998 Act.

3. 'Cookies' are text files sent to the visitor's browser by the server operating the website.

4. Data controllers should ensure that their data protection registrations ('notifications') under the Act) cover all data processing carried out – in particular, the use of personal data on the Internet.

5. *British Gas Trading Limited v. Data Protection Registrar* [1998] Info. T.L.R. 393, Data Protection Tr.; Midland Electricity Appeal, 16 Feb 2000.

CHAPTER 12

• •

International aspects

The United States

The United States continues to be one of the biggest proponents of e-commerce. US companies are increasingly looking to sell their goods and services over the Internet. For example, in 1999 it was reported that Microsoft Expedia, a US on-line travel agent, booked over US$100 million worth of travel in its first year of operation. Similarly, according to one estimate, US on-line stock traders exchanged over US$100 billion worth of securities in 1998.

In 1994, in anticipation of the tremendous demand for electronic access to goods and services, a non-profit consortium of companies called CommerceNet was created in Silicon Valley, California. CommerceNet's stated objective was (and continues to be) to promote and advance e-commerce globally.

In 1997, the US government under the Clinton administration released a report entitled *A Framework for Global Electronic Commerce,* which outlines certain basic principles intended to guide US policy regarding e-commerce.[1] This report also contains recommendations regarding tariffs and taxation, electronic payment systems and the development of a uniform commercial code for electronic commerce, as well as standards regarding intellectual property protection and privacy.

In particular, the Clinton administration has strongly urged private industry to participate with government in the analysis and formation of e-commerce policy. One example of the benefits of this partnership occurred in July 1999 when a joint statement was released by the US government and CommerceNet announcing that CommerceNet would be working with five US government agencies and several leading technology companies in order to launch a pilot project to ensure that government catalogues are accessible electronically and that the on-line systems used by the agencies are fully interoperable.

There is also much discussion and debate in the US regarding the need to establish a uniform set of laws governing electronic transactions. Several important committees have been established and are in the process of producing draft proposals but no consensus has yet been achieved.

However, a variety of federal and state laws have been enacted across the United States and these laws are already affecting the way electronic transactions are conducted. Notable federal legislation includes the No Electronic Theft Act, the Digital Millennium Copyright Act and the Children's On-Line Privacy Protection Act. Also, several US states, such as Florida, Georgia, Utah and Washington, have established laws regarding electronic signatures and records. Finally, a large body of case law has emerged in connection with various aspects of electronic transactions ranging from contract formation to fair advertising.

For companies which currently conduct or intend to conduct significant business electronically in the US or aimed at US customers, a careful analysis of the network of US federal and state laws as well as US case law is recommended.

European Union

At a European-wide level, the European Commission has issued several Directives, draft Directives and proposals applicable to e-commerce within the European Union. Their subject matter is diverse and the approach appears somewhat piecemeal. Some of these have already been discussed – for example, the Distance Selling Directive,[2] the Data Protection Directive[3] and the Directive on the use of electronic signatures[4] – all of which require EU member states to introduce national legislation to implement their provisions. Yet none of these initiatives has addressed fundamental concerns which arise when business is done electronically. None tells us how to determine whether a contract is valid or how to identify the point at which a contract is concluded on-line. They do not attempt to address secondary issues which arise in the international market, such as those of jurisdiction or liability.

The proposed Electronic Commerce Directive[5] has now been issued by the European Commission. It purports to build upon and complete the Commission's past initiatives in order to eliminate the remaining obstacles to e-commerce and to harmonise the approaches taken by individual member states.

However, the proposed Directive does not achieve its stated aims. Many issues, including those regarding contractual formation, jurisdiction and intellectual property aspects are not covered. Instead, the proposal deals with but a few of the uncertainties faced when doing business on-line, including possible exemptions from liability for ISPs and regulation of 'commercial communications' (which include certain advertising and marketing activities).

Significantly, the proposal requires all member states to conduct a qualitative review of local legislation to remove prohibitions or restrictions on the use of electronic media for all stages of the contractual process (for example, a requirement that a contract be 'in writing' or 'on paper'), including anything which might prevent the 'effective' use of electronic contracts. This obligation is said to complement the Directive on the use of electronic signatures which addresses issues concerning the legal validity of electronic signatures (but no other aspects of the legal validity of electronic contracts), as discussed above in

Chapter 8. However, it is left open to member states to exempt certain contracts (for example, those which must be registered with a public authority for validity) and it will be interesting to observe the extent to which such derogations are taken up by individual member states, particularly given the current state of play in different member states in relation to the enforceability of contracts.

Spotlight on France

E-commerce has existed in France since 1982, being the date of creation of Minitel, an on-line service including a telephone directory provided through France Telecom.

Towards the end of 1999, a new Bill was brought before the French parliament as part of the effort to modernise Internet rules. The Digital Signature Bill radically alters the legal definition of proof and offers a solution to one of the remaining barriers to development of electronic commerce in France.

The main reform is to move to end the requirement under French law that a written signature must accompany any transaction in excess of FF5,000. Digital signatures are given equal status for determining proof as that afforded to written signatures. This is subject to three conditions:

1   the person signing must be capable of being identified

2   the signature must be capable of verification; and

3   the signature must be stored in conditions that guarantee its integrity.

It is also particularly important to note the impact of general French legal principles on contracts formed on-line with customers located in France. The French Consumer Protection Code applies to on-line contracts made with consumers. Apart from rules concerning criminal liability and abuse of an ignorant or weak person (which may lead on conviction to up to five years' imprisonment and a FF60,000 penalty, and which are always applicable), the solicitation of consumers by correspondence is subject to specific consumer protection laws.

Whenever a vendor 'solicits' customers by technical means (whether by making an offer or issuing an invitation to treat), it must send written confirmation to the consumer who must then confirm his or her acceptance by returning a signed confirmation. In the absence of a signed confirmation, no obligation can be imposed on the consumer. Further, the vendor's failure to send a written confirmation may render it liable to fines and other penalties.

On the basis of general legal principles, obtaining a signed and written confirmation obviously raises difficulties in the context of Internet-based transactions. However, the new electronic signature law should clarify the matter considerably. Although the situation will be addressed further in French law through the French government's implementation of the provisions of the proposed Directives on e-commerce and use of electronic signatures, at present a 'signature' has no legal definition in France and it is unclear whether French courts would generally uphold the use of electronic or digital signatures or whether the requirement of 'writing' is satisfied by email.

However, the requirement of signed confirmation exists only in relation to 'solicitation'. Commentators are currently debating whether the passive display of goods and services on a website amounts to solicitation. Most appear to agree, however, that this is not solicitation, particularly given that in most cases, consumers access websites freely and decide whether or not to enter into an agreement to purchase.

Regardless, in any consumer contract, the consumer must be given certain details as to the products or services to be offered (including details of all corresponding prices), together with a seven-day 'cooling-off' period in which to cancel his or her order. Further, a contract in excess of FF5,000 is required to be in writing and, as discussed, it is currently uncertain as to the approach French courts will take in relation to the validity of electronic contracts in this regard. Finally, and perhaps of greatest significance, is the fact that any standard terms and conditions and disclaimers which are in English (or some other language) may not be effective, regardless of any choice of law or jurisdiction clause, as French law provides that all such terms, conditions and disclaimers in consumer contracts must be in French. It is currently being argued by some commentators that this general principle should not extend to contracts where a French consumer knowingly orders goods or services from a website operated by a supplier in a foreign jurisdiction. However, this is by no means settled.

A further development surrounds the use of English on the Internet in France. A legal action was brought by a French lobby group in 1997 against the Georgia Institute of Technology in France for creating an English-language website. Although the action was decided in the defendant's favour, this was only due to a technical defect in the plaintiff's case. As a result, the issue of linguistic obligations on the Internet remains open.

Finally, a French ISP was found liable after an action was brought by the French model Estelle Hallyday, who found ten nude photographs of herself on a site hosted by the ISP.[6] As soon as the ISP was informed of the photographs' existence, the ISP removed them and the offending site. Despite arguments that it would be impossible to police every site it hosted, the court found that, in providing an anonymous hosting service which was open to anyone, the ISP had exceeded the role of a simple transmitter of information and must assume responsibility towards third parties in certain circumstances. Hallyday was awarded the equivalent of £31,500 in damages. This case has been severely criticised and there are now plans in place to strike a sensible balance between freedom of expression and the respect of essential rights under French law.

Spotlight on Germany

After a slow start in e-commerce by comparison with other EU member states, recent market surveys suggest that Germany has the highest on-line population in Europe. Germany was also the first European country to pass legislation on digital signatures and the liability of ISPs.

In general, contracts can be concluded electronically under German law as there are no formal requirements for ordinary contracts. Certain contracts have to be made in writing (for example, tenancy agreements) but purchase contracts do not unless they are for the sale of land (in which case they must be signed in front of a notary).

Like English law, goods offered for sale on a website are unlikely to qualify as an 'offer'. Instead, German courts view a commercial website like an electronic catalogue. Therefore, it is the customer who makes the offer.

The general rule under German law is that an acceptance is only valid if it has reached the addressee. It is deemed to have been received when it reaches the 'sphere of influence' of the addressee. That is, the recipient must have the opportunity to notice the acceptance. In the physical world, this will occur when the acceptance reaches a letter box, office or answering machine. As to electronic acceptance, the relevant point in time has not yet been agreed by the German courts. The prevailing opinion to date favours a model by which an electronic acceptance is deemed to have reached the recipient when 'stored' on his or her computer. However, this might mean that the acceptance itself would need to be downloaded from the server of the relevant ISP onto the computer of the recipient to be legally valid. It is open to question whether this model will be accepted by German courts.

However, even if a contract has been formed electronically, the current position is that the mutual electronic offer and acceptance cannot be used in court as evidence for the existence of a contract. In general, German courts apply strict evidential rules which limit the admissibility of certain forms of evidence and particularly with respect to documents. At present, electronic contracts do not qualify as 'documents' under German law, particularly given that electronic documents are viewed as being susceptible to forgery. The new German Signature Act proposes to deal with this issue. Section 1(1) of the Act establishes a legal presumption that a digital signature cannot be forged. This legal presumption allows electronic declarations signed with a digital signature to be used as evidence in the so-called 'free evidence procedure'.

The German parliament is also currently considering a draft Bill to implement the Distance Selling Directive as the German Distance Selling Act. Its focus is to legislate for the level and type of compulsory information which should be provided by on-line traders, providing a right for consumers to withdraw from contracts concluded at a distance. The current version provides that certain rules found in other German legislation may prevail if they are of greater benefit to consumers.

In addition, the German Signature Act establishes a licensing system for certification authorities. It contains provisions with respect to the licensing procedure, the duties of certification authorities and their regulation. The Act also contains an important legal presumption that digital signatures (as defined by the Act) are safe. This means that messages signed with digital signatures are legally deemed to be created by the indicated author.

The German Teleservices Act, which was passed in 1997, regulates the liability of ISPs in relation to unlawful content on the Internet. However, liability (or exemption from it) depends very much on the role the ISP plays.

When offering their own content on the Internet, ISPs are fully liable for it and the general rules of liability under German law apply. If the ISPs merely host content created by others, they will only be found liable if they had actual knowledge of the unlawful content and it was possible and reasonable to prevent access to it. However, where ISPs merely provide access to content created by other people (without hosting it), they will be excluded from liability. This applies even where the ISP had knowledge of the unlawful content.

The precise scope of this legislation has not yet been clearly established by the courts and the point at which an ISP can be said to originate, host or merely provide access to content requires clarification. In addition, it is unclear as to when it would be 'reasonable' to prevent access to content and what would constitute 'actual knowledge'.

The Teleservices Act was applied for the first time in the *CompuServe* case.[7] In a decision of the court of first instance, a director of CompuServe Germany was sentenced to two years imprisonment on probation and a penalty of DM100,000 for distributing pornography over the Internet. Significantly, CompuServe Germany only provided a dial-in facility to link German customers to the US holding company. CompuServe Germany did not possess the technical means to restrict access to pornographic websites. The regional court of Munich overturned the decision and acquitted the director.

Finally, the German courts have also had occasion to consider spamming practices. In some cases, the transmission of unsolicited email has been held to be an infringement of the recipient's general privacy right. In others, it has been found that unsolicited email caused financial damage to the recipient (as the time involved in downloading and reading the message increased the user's on-line time and therefore telephone costs). Still further, some judgments have categorised spamming as unfair competition, being a nuisance to consumers.

Spotlight on Italy

No exhaustive legislation has been adopted in Italy to govern e-commerce as a whole. However, legislation with respect to the validity of certain electronic documents and digital signatures has been adopted and the Osservatorio su

Commercio Elettronico has been established to monitor e-commerce and related initiatives. The Italian government has publicly supported the view that uniform standards and solutions in specific areas affected by e-commerce must be identified. This is particularly important given the debate which currently rages with respect to contract formation, validity and jurisdiction issues regarding on-line contracts.

For example, some Italian commentators endorse the view that an on-line vendor's 'offer' does not contain all the essential elements of the contract, so that it is the customer who makes the offer (similar to an 'invitation to treat' under English law). However, others argue that the vendor in fact makes an offer to the public at large (*Offerta al Pubblico*), pursuant to Article 1336 of the Italian Commercial Code (CC).

Further uncertainty abounds with the application of general Italian legal principles regarding choice of law and jurisdiction clauses. Where goods and services are offered to Italian consumers, Italian consumer protection laws will apply to the terms of the contract and may invalidate them. In addition, Article 1341 CC may apply to business-to-business relationships. Its application may result in a court declaring a jurisdiction clause in a set of standard terms and conditions invalid on the basis that such a clause will be effective only if the other party to the contract knew or should have known of its existence (upon exercising reasonable standards of diligence). Further, some contractual clauses, including jurisdiction, limitation on liability and arbitration clauses, are not effective unless specifically approved 'in writing' – which may or may not cover email.

Spotlight on Singapore

On 10 February 1999, based largely on the UNCITRAL Model Law on Electronic Commerce, the Singapore government released the Electronic Transactions Act (ETA) and Electronic Transactions (Certification Authority) Regulations. The object of the ETA is to provide for the legal recognition of digital signatures and to provide legislative support for the acceptance of electronic filing by government agencies and statutory boards. The new laws establish a 'Commercial Code' to support e commerce transactions, outlining the rights and obligations of transacting parties and describing how a contract may be formed electronically by addressing issues of time and place of the sending and receipt of messages.

The ETA specifically provides for public key infrastructure to facilitate the use of digital signatures. Under the new law, in order for a digital signature to be recognised as a 'secure digital signature', it must be established that the digital signature was created during the operational period of a valid certificate and that the certificate was issued by a licensed Certification Authority (CA), operating in accordance with the Regulations. The role of a CA is to certify that a given public key is associated with a particular individual.

Before a CA can issue a certificate verifying a digital signature, it must ensure that the technical implementation of the digital signature is such that 'it is computationally infeasible for any person other than the person to whom the signature correlates to have created a digital signature which is verified by reference to the public key listed in that person's certificate'. This is an extremely high technical standard to satisfy.

The legislation establishes a regulatory framework for CAs to issue certificates which will allow parties participating in on-line transactions to verify the identities of the transacting parties using digital signatures registered with CAs. To cater for market demands, under the new legislation a licensed CA may issue certificates with different levels of assurance. For example, a CA may issue 'trustworthy certificates' that can create secure digital signatures, or lower-assurance certificates for simple authentication or identification purposes. Under the new laws, a party relying on the digital signature only has to show that the signature has been correctly verified and the onus is then on the other party disputing the signature to prove otherwise.

Provided that a CA has complied with the ETA and the Regulations, a CA will not be liable for any loss caused by reliance on a false or forged digital signature of a subscriber. The Regulations, however, establish extremely high technical and security thresholds which must be complied with by a CA to satisfy the legislative requirements in relation to secure digital signatures. In addition to these high technical standards, stringent financial requirements must also be satisfied before the Controller of Certification Authorities (CCA) will approve an application by a corporation to become a CA.

The CCA may require an applicant to have adequate insurance arrangements in place (to the value of at least $1 million) to cover any potential negligence claims, and in addition to have at least $2 million in paid-up capital and a combined paid-up capital and proof of available financing of not less that $5 million. The CCA will also usually require an applicant to obtain a performance bond or banker's guarantee in favour of the CCA for an amount of not less than $1 million.

However, the licensing of CAs in Singapore is recognised by the government as simply the first step in promoting the use of certification authorities. Efforts are under way to facilitate the recognition of certification from other countries. For example, Singapore and Canada have recently agreed to implement cross-certification of each other's public key infrastructure, thereby mutually recognising each other's digital certificates and certification authorities.

Finally, the ETA also clarifies the issue of an ISP's liability in relation to third-party content, ensuring that an ISP will not be liable for third-party material for which the ISP is 'merely providing access'. Under the new laws, an ISP cannot be held liable for merely providing access to third-party material. However, it must still observe and comply with the Singapore Broadcasting Authority licensing rules which regulate the provision of computer on-line services and its Internet Content Guidelines which prohibit certain types of materials (such as those that are politically sensitive or that have pornographic content). ISPs must also comply with standards set by the Telecommunications Authority of Singapore.

A note on Asia

Asian nations are now taking steps to promote and encourage the safe growth of e-commerce in the region (for example, Hong Kong, China and Malaysia). Several Asian countries, over and above Singapore, have enacted legislation aimed at regulating the activities of those seeking to do business over the Internet, resolving some of the uncertainties involved in doing business on-line and the liability of ISPs.

Notes

1. <www.ecommerce.gov/framewrk.htm> 1 July 1997.

2. Directive 97/7/EC – see Chapter 5.

3. Directive 95/46/EC – see Chapter 11.

4. Directive 99/93/EC – see Chapter 8.

5. COM (1998) 586 final – see Chapter 4.

6. *Hallyday v. Lacambre*, Cour d'Appel de Paris, 10 February 1999.

7. Local Court [Amtsgericht] Munich File No: 8340 Ds 465 17 3158/95. Decision reversed in appeal court, Landgericht Munchen I, 17 November 1999.

INDEX

advertising 46–7
  and Internet 45–6
    financial services on 49–53
Advertising Standards Authority 46
Asia, and e-commerce 69

branding 8
British Gas Trading Ltd v. Data
  Protection Registrar 59
Broadcasting Act 1990 46
Brussels Convention 15, 16

caching 21, 35
case law in USA 62
choice of law 14–15
codes of conduct, advertising 46
CommerceNet (USA) 61
compatibility 6, 7
CompuServe Inc v. Cyber Promotions
  47, 66, 69
consideration, definition 11
consumer protection 15, 16, 19
  The Distance Selling Directive
    19–20
  and EU (European Union) 19
  French Consumer Protection Code 63
  other Directives 20–21
contracts
  acceptance 12–14
    criteria for 6
  applicable laws 14–17
  concluded electronically 17, 18, 62
  consumer 15, 16
  'distance' 19–20
  The E-Commerce Directive 17–18
  electronic signatures 43
  formed electronically 18
  incorporation of terms 17
  offers/invitations to treat 11–12, 67
  on-line 14, 20

proposals causing controversy 16,
  17, 62–3
requirements 11
specification of mechanics 14, 33
support 7, 9
website-based/email 13–14
Contracts (Applicable Law) Act 1990 14
contractual disputes 15, 16
The Control of Misleading Advertise
  ments Regulations 1988 46
copyright, database rights 23, 24–5
Copyright, Designs and Patents Act
  1988 28, 29
copyright works 23–4, 28
Council of Ministers 40
customer care 9
Customs and Excise (UK) 31, 37, 39
cybersquatting 26

data, visitor 8
data protection 55–9
  The Data Protection Act 1988 55–9
  Data Protection Commissioner 58, 59
  The Data Protection Directive 20, 21,
    55, 62
  Data Protection Registrar 57, 59
  Data Protection Registry 55, 57
  Fair Processing Code 56–7
database retrieval 2
database rights 24–5
derogations
  and European Commission 18
  from The E-Commerce Directive
    17–18
Directive on the legal protection of
  computer programs 29
The Directive on Unfair Terms and
  Consumer Contracts 19, 20, 21
disclaimers
  in advertising 51

infringement
  of copyright 23–4, 28
  of trade marks 28, 29
Inland Revenue 31
integration *see* websites for business
Interceptions of Communications Act
    41, 42
International Organisation of Securities
    Commissions (IOSCO) 49, 51
Internet 1–2, 3–4
  and advertising 45 7
  and concept of permanent
    establishment 33–4
  and encryption 32, 41–2
  financial services on 49–53
  and indirect taxes 36
    liability for VAT 37–40
  and law on intention 11
  new payment mechanisms 11
  and trade marks 25
Internet Corporation for Assigned
    Names and Numbers (ICANN)
    26, 27
Internet Protocol (IP) 3, 26
Internet Service Providers *see* ISPs
Internet Tax Freedom Act 1998 (USA)
    36
Investment Management Regulatory
    Organisation (IMRO) 52
IOSCO (International Organisation of
    Securities Commissions) 49, 51
IP (Internet Protocol) 3, 26
ISPs (Internet Service Providers) 5
  and acceptance of contracts 14
  acting as conduits 52
  arranging deals in investments 52–3
  and concept of permanent
    establishment 34–5, 38
  contracts concluded electronically 18
  and encryption 41
  in European Union 62
  in Germany 66
  liability of information society 21
  and personal data 58
  server response 7
  in Singapore 68–9
  and VAT 40
  see also on-line service provision
Italy, and e-commerce 66–7

key escrow 41

liability
  non-contractual 16

product 46
  of service providers 21, 62, 66, 68
licences, and indemnities 6
linking 27–9
Lotteries & Amusements Act 1976 47
Lugano Convention 15

Marks and Spencer plc and Others v.
    One in a Million Ltd 26, 29
m-commerce 2
mirror sites 35
The Misleading Advertising Directive
    20, 21

OECD (Organisation for Economic
    Co-operation and Development)
  Model Convention 33, 36
  Model Treaty 33, 34
  and taxation 31, 35, 36, 39, 40
Office of Fair Trading 46
on-line service provision 2
  and VAT 38, 39
  see also ISPs
Organisation for Economic
    Co-operation and Development
    see OECD
Ottawa Conference 31
packet-switch technology 3
passing-off action 28, 29
portals 8
Prince plc v. Prince Sportswear Group
    Inc 26, 29
public key 42, 67, 68

registration
  international, of domain names 26–7
  proposals for non-EU service
    providers 39
  of trade marks 25
Rome 2 Regulation 16
Rome Convention 14
search engines 8
searches *see* websites for business,
    rights clearances
SEC (Securities and Exchange
    Commission) 51
security 7
  see also electronic signatures
servers *see* ISPs
Shetland Times Limited v. Wills 28, 29
Singapore
  Certification Authorities 67–8
  and e-commerce 67–9